M103- No Apologize
for worship, Be
saying Justifying why
we clap, Dance is being
Ashamed / Apologizing.

Adoption
Love &
Letters

Edward William Herman

ANOINTED
Quill
Publications

Adoption, Love & Letters

by Edward William Herman

Printed in the United States of America.
ISBN 1-58169-146-7

To Order *Adoption, Love & Letters* **Online, Go to:**

www.anointedquill.com

ANOINTED Quill Publications

You can contact Edward William Herman at:
Anointed Quill Publications

Edward & Paula Herman
601 E. Main Street
Reedsburg, WI 53959
(608) 524-1111 eherman@charter.net

Deepest Gratitude and Thanks to. . .

- My editors: Dede S., Lois G., Suzanne F, and especially, Sandy K. (Sandy, want some Peanut Butter Pie?) You've all been a blessing of priceless proportion to this work. If it wasn't for your painstaking efforts, I'd still have my *T's* dotted and my *I's* crossed! (I haven't had this much correction since I was a kid!)

- My pastor, Rev. Jack E. Yonts II: Your training, encouragement, support, example, and investment in my life and ministry is more precious than gold. Thank you for blessing me. I count you as one of my life's most valued assets.

- My brothers, Joe and David: for your invaluable help and support in this project, for your unconditional acceptance of me in your lives, and for your unselfish willingness to share with me one of your most precious treasures—your mother.

- My adoptive parents, Martha and (late) Donald Herman: for unconditionally loving me at times when I was unlovable, for raising me as your own, and for allowing this miracle story to take place. I'll never be able to repay you for the life you gave me. Don't ever forget—you'll *always* be Mom and Dad to me.

- The joys of my life—my sons, Jordan and Jonathan: Thank you for the patience and longsuffering you showed toward that ornery guy sitting at the computer for the past six months (You remember him?— the one constantly saying, *"Shhhh, shhhh!"*). You are two of the finest little Christian gentlemen I've ever seen. I'm proud of you, I'm blessed by you, I thank God for you, and I love you—eternally.

- My precious wife and best friend, Paula: for toiling beside me many long hours during this project (Honey, can you say "Copy, Paste, and Edit?") We hurt, we rejoiced, but by the grace of God, first we lived it, then we wrote it—together. I love you more than language can express. Thank you, my friend, for eighteen wonderful years. The honeymoon keeps on going . . .

- Jesus Christ: All that I am and all that I will be is because of You.

Dedicated to. . .

- Every soul winner and those aspiring to be such, who, with diligence and longsuffering, have faithfully toiled in prayer and sown in tears for the sake of souls, and perhaps, at times, have found themselves becoming weary in well doing: that you may know the extent to which God can and will redirect the order of life, positioning you to be used for His glory so that you may go forth with weeping, bearing precious seed, in boldness and confidence—doubtless, knowing that when you come again it will be with rejoicing, bringing your sheaves with you.

> *Therefore, my beloved brethren, be ye steadfast, unmovable, always abounding in the work of the Lord, forasmuch as ye know that your labor is not in vain in the Lord.*
>
> *1 Corinthians 15:58*

- Every person who carries the burden of a broken and hurting heart, whose purpose in this life eludes them, and whose fate in the life to come is uncertain, and who knows not the boundless love of God: that you might come to realize the extent to which Jesus Christ reaches for your heart and longs to restore the years of your life that hardship and heartache have stolen from you, and that you might diligently seek Him with all your heart, soul, mind, and strength so He may eternally reward you with joy unspeakable.

> *But as it is written, Eye hath not seen, nor ear heard, neither have entered into the heart of man, the things which God hath prepared for them that love him.*
>
> *1 Corinthians 2:9*

- The greatest earthly blessing in my life—my precious family: Paula, Jordan and Jonathan

- My Lord and Savior, Jesus Christ, who has given me a testimony to share, that through the telling of which, proper glory may be given to His Name.

Foreword

O ver the course of my ministry I have been blessed to see my share of miracles. In fact, I have experienced some tremendous miracles myself. It seems that some miracles occur of their own accord and others—well—they require our involvement. What you are about to read is a miracle story. It's a story of a family whose faith in God carried them into the realm of the miraculous. It's a story of love, loss, separation, reunion and sorrow turned to joy. It is a detailed account of how one young lady faced with a difficult choice, chose wisely, setting into motion a chain of events that would span a period of thirty-eight years, cross the continental United States, and ultimately affect generations.

Having known the Hermans for over a decade and pastored them for almost as long, this whole account should not have come as a surprise because these are truly exceptional people. But to be honest, it did. For me, the story starts, sitting on a wooden bench across from my good friend at our favorite barbeque place. After a few questions about the adoption process my wife and I had recently gone through, a plate full of ribs and a pile of used napkins, nothing seemed too far out of the ordinary. Little did I know that I was about to be granted a front row seat in God's theatre of the miraculous. Had I been listening, surely I would have heard the orchestra tuning up, because this presentation came complete with its own symphony—the score, *How Great Thou Art.* I watched in wonder as the curtain lifted and God revealed the stage where He was about to direct the drama of a lifetime. As the lights came up, the characters, Marilyn, Ed, Paula and many others in their supporting roles, began to move flawlessly under the hand of God's direction.

You might expect to find a story like this played out on Broadway or in a fairy tale. As you read *Adoption, Love & Letters*, remember, it is a God story. When I read the completed manuscript for the first time, I was moved deeply and reminded of the greatness of the grace of

God. So, as you turn the page, prepare to be captivated and drawn into the lives of Marilyn, Ed and Paula. Get ready to cry, laugh out loud, feel the pain of loss and celebrate the ultimate victory as the pages almost turn themselves. *Adoption, Love & Letters* is a true story, a wonderful story, about great people and a great God.

Jack E. Yonts II, Senior Pastor
Pentecostals of the Fox Cites
Menasha, Wisconsin

Introduction

J esus Christ told us very plainly in Matthew 7:7-8 to *ask, and it shall be given you; seek, and ye shall find; knock, and it shall be opened unto you: For every one that asketh receiveth; and he that seeketh findeth; and to him that knocketh it shall be opened.* If I have ever read a book that fulfilled this scripture, it is *Adoption, Love & Letters.*

Ed Herman has penned his heart in wondering, longing, seeking, and finding a true desire from within, which our Lord promised that He would fulfill. I believe everyone that read's this work will feel Ed's passion for the answer to the mystery of his biological roots. I believe all will be deeply moved as you discover how God brings forth Ed's answer and how He weaves a beautiful tapestry of life's relationships within the Herman family.

I have known the Herman family for the last four years, and I don't know of a more dedicated family to the cause of Christ and to the cause of lasting relationships. Please, sit down and open this book as you would a family picture album. Let the drama unfold, and let the wonderment of God's special gift—His love—take hold of your own heart as you read *Adoption, Love & Letters.*

Rev. John E. Putnam
Wisconsin District Superintendent
United Pentecostal Church International

Dear Ed,

...There is a theory I've heard that says that when a child is born and the mother and child meet and touch and interact, a bond is formed, a special kind of connection is made in those first minutes/hours/days. I guess, as a mother, I can believe that.

But, I was wondering, what if the mother and child DON'T meet, touch, or interact when the child is born? What happens if that first meeting takes place 34 1/2 years later? Did they miss the opportunity for that bond to be formed, or was it just delayed until they DO meet, touch, and interact?

The reason I question this is because when we met in person, I felt something special for you—a connection, a bond. From that moment on, you were never a stranger to me. I didn't know all the details about you, but I knew YOU and loved YOU. Do you know what I mean? Did you feel it, too? Or maybe you felt it all along, all these years, and I just now caught up.

I love you, Ed, in a way reserved only for you. The bond is there, and it's as strong as if it had been there forever.

Love, Marilyn

Prologue

1 t was a typically beautiful spring day in Cape Canaveral, Florida—a perfect opportunity to launch another chapter in the short but storied history of United States space exploration. Liftoff of Apollo 13 came at 2:13 p.m. on April 11, 1970 without major incident. Intended to be the third Apollo mission to put a man on the moon, it had a crew of three: Commander James A. Lovell and pilots Fred Haise, Jr. and John L. Swigert, Jr. Morale was high in the spacecraft and at mission control in Houston. It seemed the Apollo 13 mission would ultimately be a NASA success.

But fifty-five hours into the flight, a warning system indicated low pressure in hydrogen tank one. After receiving instructions from mission control to turn on the cryogenic fans and heaters, the crew heard a loud bang. Gauges now revealed dangerously low voltage conditions, prompting Swigert to utter the now-famous under-statement of all time: "Okay, Houston . . . we've got a problem here." Apollo 13 was in trouble.

An electrical short circuit had occurred in oxygen tank two of the service module due to damaged wires on the fan motor, causing the tank to explode. The situation now in the command module, *Odyssey*, was so critical that mission control ordered it shutdown. Without electrical output from its fuel cells, the command module was abandoned and the crew moved into the lunar module. Within three hours the *Odyssey* lost all oxygen, water, and electrical power, as well as the ability to use its propulsion system.

The dilemma was complicated by a risky plan required to get the wounded spacecraft home. The lunar module, *Aquarius*, whose engines were intended only for a lunar landing, was going to have to provide the thrust needed to boost the craft into a free-return trajectory. The plan, in theory, was quite simple: the first engine burn would put them on course to circle around the moon, and the second burn would cut precious time off the trip to ensure their supplies held out. The world watched televised broadcasts of the unfolding drama in rapt attention to see what the fate of the crew would be. Timing and execution were critical. Apollo 13 had only one chance to get it right.

On April 17, 1970 Apollo 13 splashed down in the South Pacific, the entire crew safely home. The splashdown, it has been said, was one of the closest ever to the recovery ship, nearly hitting the deck. The annuls of modern space exploration record that Apollo 13, with the help of its engineers, the bravery of its astronauts, and the prayers of a nation, birthed a life-saving miracle. It was a small window of opportunity in a finite moment in time, a narrow chance for salvation, with life and death hanging in the balance.

Such is the story of Marilyn, my birth mother, my friend—the woman who gave me life. I was approximately twelve years old when I learned that I was adopted. While growing up, it caused me little concern to know that I had a mysterious past. Then it was simply a fact of life—I was adopted. But a series of events starting when I was 18 eventually culminated with the meeting of my birth mother after a thirty-four year separation that began at my birth. From the first meeting, our relationship took off as spectacularly as the liftoff of Apollo 13, soaring quickly to unimaginable heights of love and affection. With it came great excitement for the future as well as unexpected problems, hurdles and heartaches. It was a fairy tale, but nobody expected nor could have predicted how short it would last.

Nonetheless, this is a story of a miracle —or maybe I should say, *miracles*—miracles of emotional healing, deliverance, forgiveness, thanksgiving, and last-chance salvation—just to name a few. It's a story of how the desire to have answers to life-long questions produced unexpected revelations, occurring against all odds, defying human logic and reasoning, leaving behind a testimony of what can happen when we have faith in God and diligently seek after Him. It goes beyond the beauty of a reunion between a child and his mother.

It transcends the finite ability of what human love can do and illustrates the awesome and unlimited power of love divine.

Maybe you don't believe that God can perform the impossible. Perhaps you don't believe the incredible because the incredible has never happened to you. Well then, sit back, get comfortable, and get ready to turn the page. You are about to read what can happen when God executes His perfect will at just the right point in a person's life. Throughout this book you will read, in Marilyn's own words—lest you think the author's account to be too exaggerated—excerpts from dozens of e-mails and letters written by her, the one who received these miracles at the precise time in her life when she needed them most.

For as it was with the miracle of Apollo 13, every event had to come to pass perfectly in the fullness of time if this story was to ever be written, every step divinely ordained by God, all taking place within a brief chapter in time. It was a small window of opportunity for the extraordinary. This, too, is a story of miracles. This is Marilyn's story.

Edward William Herman

Chapter 1

December 8, 1999
Menasha, Wisconsin

*A*s I sat downstairs in the den, alone in the dark, I felt a little foolish, the room deathly still and quiet; but I could not bring myself to do anything else. The only sound that could be heard was my wife Paula, scurrying around upstairs performing some last-minute straightening of the house, propelled by an increasing nervous energy. Thoughts and memories raced through my mind at breakneck speed, like watching a videotape stuck on fast-forward. At that moment I felt scatter-brained, to say the least. After all, how can a person possibly recall, much less appraise, thirty-four years of one's own life in a matter of mere minutes. Yet, that is exactly what I found myself attempting to do, while impatiently waiting for six o'clock to come. Every minute dragged on as if the hour hand, attempting to reach twelve, was burdened by some invisible force bent on prolonging my anxiety by holding back time.

It was hard to believe that this momentous event in my life would finally come to pass. My birth mother, Marilyn, was scheduled to ring *my* doorbell on this cold, late-autumn night in December at precisely six o'clock sharp. Up to this point I had never met nor spoken to her, yet some innate intuition told me that she was punctual without exception.

"I see headlights coming around the corner. I think she's here," Paula called out as she peered through the blinds. "Are you going to want me to answer the door?"

"Yes," I replied in monotone, suddenly paralyzed by fear and wondering what in the world possessed me to pursue this whole endeavor in the first place. Fortunately, we didn't have the boys to worry about. Jordan, seven, and Jonathan, four, by pre-agreement with Marilyn, would not be present, having been shipped off earlier to Grandma Gail's house. Glancing at my watch, I noticed it was indeed six o'clock—right on the money.

True, it was cowardly of me to expect Paula to shoulder the burden of greeting Marilyn at the door without me, but I reckoned I was in this situation largely because of her. It was Paula, spurred on by her own curiosity regarding my adoption and completely helpless to fight against her own tenacious personality, that was responsible for arranging this meeting. She had acted as the intermediary between Marilyn and me. It was Paula who called her on the phone a little over a week before, setting in motion a whole chain of events. It was because of that phone call that Marilyn had requested a letter from me and pictures of the entire family, which she had received less than twenty-four hours ago. It's not that I was blaming Paula; on the contrary, had it been solely up to me, this meeting would not have stood a chance. I might have been content to live life as I'd known it, never pursuing answers to the unknowns of my origin. I felt bad, but for the time being, she was going to have to go it alone. I not only felt justified, but desperately in need of a few extra minutes to pull myself together before seeing Marilyn face-to-face.

Scarcely breathing, I waited for the sound of the doorbell, but it wasn't coming. The minutes passed; and although I wasn't ready to ascend from my "sanctuary", I was beginning to wonder why nothing was happening.

"She's not getting out of her car!" Paula cried, with excitement rising in her voice. Looking out the window, she continued to give a running commentary on what was happening out in the driveway (or, in this case, what was not happening).

"She's just sitting in her car with the lights on!"

I couldn't think how to respond to that, so I simply sat there and said nothing. I'm not sure what Paula expected me to do, but I certainly had no intention of running out to this person's car saying, "Please come in. Don't be afraid; we're both in here freaking out just like you are!"

Paula was now starting to get frustrated, wondering why I wouldn't answer her or come upstairs. Not only that, but what was Paula supposed to say when, after finally opening the door for this woman, she's standing there without me? She was even more afraid that Marilyn might have a change of heart and leave before we could meet her. Neither of us was prepared for this panic and raw emotion. Perhaps a simple discussion ahead of time of what roles we would each perform would have helped, but one thing was clear: we were quickly learning that there is no instruction manual for a situation like this. But Paula and I weren't the only ones feeling anxious . . .

Marilyn's letter to her friend, Lori—

...We arranged to meet at their house that night without their children present.

By the time I left home to go to their house, I had shaking hands and my heart was pounding. I sat in the car in their driveway for a long time before I got out of the car, knowing that this would change my life, one way or another...

When the doorbell finally rang, I was still downstairs picturing a faceless woman entering my house, and wishing I could observe from a hidden vantage point. Answering the door, Paula immediately felt a stab of panic. Marilyn was trim and had a fashionable haircut. She was dressed stylishly in a white cashmere turtleneck sweater, a black skirt, and black pumps. Paula had seen Marilyn in person a few years prior at a sports banquet and had an image in her mind of the woman that would come to the door. But the person walking into the house had obviously changed. Could we have made a mistake? It didn't seem possible. We had thoroughly and meticulously done our homework and knew without a doubt, this had to be the right person.

Marilyn was visibly nervous. Neither of them was comfortable enough to offer a hug or even an enthusiastic "Hello," so Paula just stepped back, tentatively smiled, and let her in the door. Marilyn began to scan the room behind her, presumably looking for me.

"Oh, he'll be right up," Paula said, reading the questioning look on her face. "He's downstairs."

Meanwhile, as murmurs of uneasy greetings were now being exchanged upstairs, I still couldn't bring myself to move. After a few minutes, I sensed an uncomfortable silence as the pleasantries were coming to an end and decided I had better go rescue my wife. *Well, this is it,* I thought. *Move Ed. Just move.*

It only took ten seconds to climb the stairs to the living room, but it felt like ten hours of hard labor. When I got to the top step, Marilyn was standing in the middle of the room. With a sharp intake of breath, she stopped talking in mid-sentence and froze the instant our eyes met. She stared without blinking for a few seconds, waiting for me to make the first move. This was one of those rare moments you sometimes imagine yourself being in. You know the kind— where you rehearse a scene over and over in your mind and pretend that at the most climactic moment you utter something profound and amazing because you know the importance that a first impression makes? It was then that I dramatically spread my arms wide, palms facing upward, as if to silently announce, "Ta-da!" Wow, what an impression! You'd think with thirty-four years to prepare, I could have come up with something better than that! The only thing missing was the drum roll.

Marilyn's letter to her friend, Lori—

...Paula answered the door looking even more beautiful than in the picture. She and I hardly spoke, both of us so nervous. And as I walked into their living room, Ed was coming up the stairs from a lower level. I stopped for a few seconds to look closely at him and walked right into his arms. My first face-to-face contact with him was a hug...

It was ironic that I could feel so speechless when there was so much to say. Not to mention that here I was, hugging a complete stranger, waiting for some kind of instantaneous bonding to magically occur between us. I kept trying to convince myself that this was indeed my birth mother. *I came from this woman!* For many years I was accustomed to thinking of myself as a lone entity with no knowledge of who created me and no heritage to attach myself to. I grew up not looking like anybody in my adoptive family and was reconciled to the fact that I would never have anybody to identify with, physically or historically. Now here I was with the opportunity to finally make that connection, and all I could do was wrestle with an overwhelming sense of feeling like an actor performing a part in a drama. One thing, though, was for sure: she gave a great bear hug!

When we separated, Marilyn, with her neck craned forward and her eyes squinted, peered intensely into my face.

"Can you take off your glasses, please?" she requested.

I took them off and she studied me harder. Then she began to slowly circle around me, scanning up and down, returning to stand directly in front of me. It was a little unnerving to be so closely scrutinized, yet I wasn't annoyed by it. I was trying to understand what it must have been like for her to be looking for the first time into the eyes of the person that she had carried and given birth to. I will say, however, at that moment I became keenly aware of what the inhabitants of the monkey cage at the zoo must feel!

"You don't look like anybody I know," she announced with finality.

I was slightly confused by her comment but didn't ask her to clarify it. *Who knows?* Maybe it simply meant that she half-expected to recognize me because we had lived in the same city for over thirty years. Paula wondered, on the other hand, if perhaps we did *indeed* have the wrong person. Later, we came to find out that there proved to be a good reason for her close scrutiny.

Marilyn and I sat down on the couch together, positioned so we could face each other. Paula, making herself inconspicuous so as not to be intrusive, took a seat across the room slightly off to one side.

Marilyn's letter to her friend, Lori—

...Lori, it was the most unbelievable experience, sitting on the

sofa next to this person who was a stranger, yet NOT a stranger. He looks a lot like Joe [Marilyn's son—my half-brother], although I didn't realize it that first night. All I knew was that he DIDN'T look like who I thought he would look like. It had never, ever occurred to me that he would look different from the way I had always imagined he would. It had never, ever occurred to me that there would be some of ME in him.

"I know you both have lots of questions, and that you, Ed, have questions about your father," Marilyn continued, mindful that we were certain to have a myriad of things to ask her.

"I know his name, so it wasn't a situation like that," she said. "Someday I'll tell you more about him, but not tonight. And one thing I'll never do is tell you his name."

As she spoke, it was clear from Marilyn's countenance that whoever and whatever this man was, he was a topic that deeply troubled her. When pondering the issue of my biological parents over the years, I never had a burning desire to know about my biological father. Despite that, seeing the anguished look on her face and considering the possibilities of what put it there, speculation definitely began to blow on the embers of my curiosity.

"Let me reassure you, first of all, that that's not something I've ever really been interested in," I said, hoping to put her at ease. "You are free to tell me anything you want to or nothing at all. I'll be fine with that. I know you might find this hard to believe, me being adopted and all," I continued, "but I don't believe an adopted person necessarily has an absolute *right* to know their background."

Legally, I had no right to know. Marilyn gave me up under the laws of that day, laws that were supposed to ensure the protection of everyone's privacy. Any information I gleaned would only come from her bestowing me with the right to learn of my heritage.

Marilyn seemed surprised by my opinion but had no way of knowing about an incident that took place many years earlier while I was searching for her which helped to formulate my view on this particular subject. She must have felt safer because she decided to go a little deeper with the topic.

"It was a situation where he never knew about you at all," Marilyn proceeded to explain. "I don't remember much at all about that time in my life or how long I was with him, only that it was in late summer of 1964."

The trust between us was starting to build, causing her to struggle with how much to reveal—on the one hand, not wanting to deny me, but on the other, not wanting to compromise the years of effort it took to deeply bury the memory of this painful time in her life.

"He was the type of person that…"

"Wait, wait, just a second," I interrupted. "Before you say anything, I want to tell you how I've always pictured him, to see if I've been right." She paused and then nodded that it was okay for me to continue.

"First of all, was he a heavy drinker?" I asked.

Marilyn cast her eyes downward and slowly nodded.

"For all these years," I began, "I've pictured him as a mean person with a violent temper, someone who couldn't hold a job and who wasn't very smart—just an awful person."

As I talked, Marilyn's face became red and her eyes welled up with tears.

"I've always thought that he did you wrong and that you got the raw end of the deal."

It looked as if each comment struck her like a punch in the stomach. She slowly shook her head back and forth, lowering it down into her chest. I reached over and took her hand in mine. I had said enough.

"How could you know these things?" Marilyn asked, her face a mixture of sadness and astonishment.

"I'm not sure," I answered, shocked as well that I had so accurately hit the mark. "I guess I always had a gut-feeling that he wasn't a very nice man."

We continued to hold each other's hand for quite awhile, all three of us trying to absorb all that had been said. One could sense a bond between us now beginning to form.

"I always pictured you much differently, though," I went on to say. "Even before I knew about you, I pictured you, in my mind, as a beautiful woman with long hair, but I was never able to see your face. I placed you on kind of a pedestal, held you in high regard," I said, pausing to summon the image back to my mind.

"I guess I was so grateful that you didn't choose to abort me that I saw you as this virtuous woman, committed to doing the right thing, no matter how bad the circumstance. And because of that, even though I never knew you, I've always loved you."

After taking a second to absorb that, Marilyn said, "I also want to apologize to both of you for how I treated you when Paula called eight years ago. There were situations going on in my life at that time that were very stressful, and it was not a good time for me." (Marilyn was referring to a decision that Paula and I made to contact her in 1991. We had decided to have children and, inevitably, the question of my medical history came up.)

"You called at a time when my husband, Danny, had just found out that he had terminal cancer—and my son, David, was struggling because a close friend had recently committed suicide."

Neither Paula nor I harbored any hard feelings toward Marilyn over that phone call, although it was a little difficult for me for a few days afterward because I had been caught off guard by her response.

"Marilyn, you really don't owe us an explanation," Paula said.

"Yes I do," she insisted. "I feel bad that I said what I did, but the only thing I felt was terror when I realized what the call was about."

"Well, I want you to know, straight from me, that I'm not angry about it and I accept your apology," I assured her. "I'm just glad we got the chance to meet tonight."

To continue on a more positive note, we agreed to a moratorium on the subject of "him," as he became referred to. So with the emotionally heavy stuff aside, for the moment, at least, we were free to catch up on the last thirty-four years. I told her about the family I was adopted into: my mom and dad and two younger brothers, Mike and Jim. I chronicled my life up to the present—my accomplishments as well as my shortcomings. Much of what I said revolved around our involvement with church because it had come to be such a significant part of our lives.

Marilyn did much the same and talked about the years she was married to Danny and about her two sons (my half-brothers): Joe, twenty-nine, and David, twenty-five. Throughout the evening, Paula caught her, more than once, glancing up at our family picture hanging on the living room wall. The picture was a couple of years old so the kids were quite young. In it, Jordan is handsomely dressed in a suit and tie and looks like a little man. He has the sweetest smile on his face and always stands out with his red hair. Jonathan is sitting on Paula's lap with a cute smile, a patented twinkle in his eyes, and the fattest, plumpest, most kissable cheeks you've ever laid your lips on. Not officially having had any grandchildren until tonight, that picture must have provoked a lot of thoughts for Marilyn!

It was when everyone was feeling more at ease with each other that Marilyn addressed Paula in a more serious manner. With her brow furrowed, she asked, "What made you decide to call me the day you did?" referring to the latest phone call.

"Well, if you *really* want to know the answer to that, I'll tell you," she replied with some hesitation. "I feel like God *told* me to call you."

Both Paula and I wanted to be careful with what we said to Marilyn the first time meeting. Although we have never been ashamed about what God has done in our lives, we didn't want to be perceived as "preaching" to her. Experiencing the miraculous change that God had brought to our lives about ten years earlier made us zealous to share our testimony with others, but we also wanted Marilyn to see that we were still "regular" people.

She hesitated a moment, trying to absorb the implication of what Paula said. It's not that she didn't want to believe Paula, but it looked like Marilyn was thinking there had to be a more logical explanation. Seizing the opportunity to explain, Paula told Marilyn the story of how she found herself picking up the phone that November morning—beyond her own logic and human reasoning—dialing Marilyn's number without any forethought as to what she would say. Marilyn listened politely but still didn't seem totally convinced.

"But why did it happen on that specific day? If you would have called six months ago, two months ago, or even two weeks ago, I probably would have responded the same way I did the last time you called."

"Again, I felt God wanted me to call you, *right then,*" Paula reiterated.

Marilyn insisted on trying to understand what truly motivated Paula to act so spontaneously. We realized from earlier in our conversation that spiritual topics were neither mentioned nor readily apparent in Marilyn's life, so we both wondered why she seemed so determined to understand. It wasn't until later that we would learn the incredible reason it interested her so much.

"Why don't we go downstairs to the den so you can look at our family pictures?" Paula suggested.

As was the case upstairs, the photos of the boys arrested Marilyn's attention, particularly the ones from when they were infants.

We had covered a lot of ground together. The night was winding down on a good note, but all three of us were getting tired and starting to come down off the adrenaline rush from the last few hours. While we were standing in the middle of the room, Marilyn turned and stared at me again. We momentarily froze, looking at each other, then responded with another long, hard hug.

After we pulled apart I asked the question, "So, where do we go from here?"

"Well, I *definitely* don't want it to end here," she said.

"You know, Marilyn, like I told you on the phone, you can have as much of us as you want, or as little. We will not pressure you at all. You call the shots." Paula reassured her. She seemed pleased by the lack of expectation on our part.

It was getting late, and we went back upstairs so she could get ready to leave. Marilyn said, "I would like to be included in your lives. But I have to tell you—the God stuff is not a part of your lives that I'll be involved with."

When she said that, the impact of her statement hit me squarely in the face. It suddenly dawned on me the magnitude of what had all taken place this night. *God must be getting ready to do something awesome!* It's not that I didn't think about it before, but I had all I could do to sort out the thoughts and emotions of meeting her for the first time. With that completed, thinking of the spiritual possibilities for this relationship as well, made me feel giddy on the inside. I then pulled off an "academy-award winning" job of not revealing the excitement and anticipation surging through me.

"That's fine, Marilyn. There're no strings attached," I said calmly, nodding my head sincerely. But as I spoke the words, my mind was thinking, *Lady, if you only understood what God has miraculously done to orchestrate this meeting! You have no idea of the miracle that's about to happen here!*

Marilyn's letter to her friend, Lori—

...The three of us spent three hours together, talking, answering each other's questions and shaking off the nerves. I can't say I was comfortable and relaxed, but I wasn't uncomfortable.

They treated me just as they had in Paula's phone call and Ed's letter, with gentleness, consideration for my feelings and reassurance that I had nothing to fear. There was never any pressure or assumption that this would go further than this one meeting.

Ed had questions, most of which I answered before he could ask them, about his father, but his questions were only out of curiosity, not any desire to contact or meet him. He told me what he thought were the circumstances surrounding his birth, and he had it down perfectly, even though he had no way of knowing any of that. He assured me he had no regrets or resentment toward me, only gratitude that I gave him life. I still marvel that it's true, but now I know it is...

Chapter 2

June 8, 1965
Green Bay, Wisconsin

*I*n keeping with the arrangements made by Catholic Social
Services, I was swept away from my mother immediately after
birth. She was never given the opportunity to see me, which
was deemed reasonable considering the circumstances: she was
about to give me up for adoption. I weighed in at a modest 6 lbs. 4
oz., and was 20 inches long—a bit small if one is aspiring to be a
heavyweight boxer, no doubt, but not too bad for your average baby
boy.

One week after my birth, Father Burkhardt, a Catholic priest,
drove to Green Bay and took my prospective parents, Donald and
Martha Herman, from the village of Combined Locks, to meet me.
The couple had been married for almost seven years and had been
trying desperately to have children, but to no avail. Their doctor had
ultimately recommended that they adopt because the diagnosis
concluded they had no chance of having their own children.

Without delay, they had begun the process to adopt a child in
September of 1964 and were recently told that a potentially suitable
infant had just been born. The nationalities of the child's biological
parents were similar to the Herman's, which was important—as it
was customary in that day to match a baby as closely as possible to
the adopting parents. Hence, this particular day found the Hermans
on their way to meet a baby boy they might decide to adopt. (Thank
God, for my sake that the meeting went well!)

Evidently I must not have cried out too unnecessarily, or kicked
up too much fuss because Martha left with her mind made up: I was
the child they wanted. (I say only somewhat tongue-in-cheek. Had

they been able to see into the future, they might have thought better of their decision—I would prove to be a real handful in the coming years!) Notwithstanding, my short stint without a mom and dad was about to come to an end.

Almost two weeks later, the agency felt obliged to dutifully name me and have me baptized Catholic at a local church. I was cared for by foster parents for the next four weeks until the time my adoption could be completed. On July 15, 1965, my new mother and new Great Aunt Phyllis picked me up to take me home (my new father, by a cruel twist of fate, was not able to get off work).

For years to come I was to hear the story of how my mom, inexplicably, had wrapped me in many stifling blankets on that hot and humid summer day, supposedly to prevent me from catching a "chill!" Aunt Phyllis still wonders to this day how in the world I was able to breathe at all!

Five years later we settled in Appleton, Wisconsin, in an area known as the "Fox Cities". With a population of just over two hundred thousand people, it has always been a strong economic community with steady growth, even during times of national economic downturn. It also boasts of having the largest concentration of paper mills anywhere in the country. As the Fox River meanders through a rolling landscape of dairy farmland, it is dotted along the way by many small cities and towns, often connected one-to-another, each retaining their own unique character, with Appleton being the largest. Appleton's low crime rate, good schools, and upper Midwest personality made it a nice place for me to grow up.

Our house was on Lindbergh Street, an unpaved "thoroughfare" when we moved there in 1970, located on the north side of town where the growing city continued to stretch out, taking over the surrounding farmland. Directly behind us were undeveloped fields that, to a little kid, seemed to go on forever. It was in these wide open fields of long grass that I learned to play baseball and football, mouse hunt, roll giant snowballs, build forts, make friends and enemies, and mischievously, play with matches.

Two years after I was brought home, my short tenure as an only child ended surprisingly with the (presumably impossible) birth of my brother, Mike. Unlike me, he was not adopted. It seems that doctors, like weathermen, are granted the leeway to be wrong on occasion, and in this particular case, fully exercised that right— twice! Another two years later, again much to the surprise of my mom and dad, my brother, Jim, was added to the family. Go figure.

My mom was a strong presence in our house. She grew up on Long Island, New York and had a strong east coast personality to match her accent. She was as protective of us kids as she was firm. My former pastor once said that she "loves fiercely." It was true. There was never a moment growing up where I doubted her love for me, always accepting me as if I were the fruit of her own womb. Of course, this is a credit to her because I gave Mom plenty of opportunity to want to disown me by employing a myriad of creative ways to cause trouble.

My Dad was a relatively short man with a husky build. He seemed bigger than he was because he was broad across the shoulders and had thick arms. Dad always wore a fifties-style crew cut. As far back as I can remember, he was a patrolman with the Appleton Police Department. He greatly influenced my childhood dream of one day becoming a police officer. Although that never happened, I would eventually get my college degree in criminal justice, but ended up finding my calling in sales.

Dad had grown up and lived in the Fox Cities his whole life, other than his time in the military. He was a quiet man in a crowd, but he could carry on a conversation for hours if you got him one-on-one—particularly if the subject revolved around hunting, fishing, firearms, or, of course, politics. His sense of humor was very disarming, especially to kids who most of the time saw him carrying a gun!

Mike grew up to have the same physique as Dad. Short and stocky in build, with the same large forearms and broad back and sandy blond hair that eventually turned brown. Like my father, Mike has a quiet personality. He is also the one in the family most ready to lend a hand to someone else.

Jim was built much the same way I was: thin and bony, although the similarity was not due to genetics in our case. Everybody knew

Jimmy for his red hair—his signature feature. He had more of Mom's physical features, although the irony was that none of us really looked like each other—me being the only one, in this case, that had an excuse. I've been told on many occasions that Jim worshipped me while growing up. It was too bad for him—he probably could've picked a better role model! My influence eventually led him down some of the same rough roads that I would traverse.

My brothers endured me—even though I was a tyrant. Domineering and overbearing, I bordered on being cruel. One time, as the story goes, I had just come home from the store wearing a new pair of shoes and proceeded to kick Mike in the mouth, who at the time, was crawling on the floor. I don't have the heart or the patience to try to psychoanalyze why I was such an insufferable little punk. Maybe it's because I had low self-esteem and a lack of confidence, making me feel awkward. I wasn't a geek, just paranoid and unsure of every step I took. It's not that I wasn't smart in school; I just didn't have the confidence to do well. It's not that I wasn't athletic in sports; I just didn't have the confidence to play. It's not that I didn't like life; I was just unsure of the rules for living!

For example, it was a miracle that I joined the Pop Warner football team in seventh grade because I *never* participated in organized sports. My fearfulness earned me the dubious honor of third string offensive guard. I wore jersey number 19. Perchance you don't understand the game of football, let me explain: if you're assigned the number 19 as an offensive lineman, you're so far down the depth chart that they have to file a missing person's report just to locate you on the player list! At a measly seventy-five pounds, my physique was more suited to that of a backup punter; but the coaches were obligated by league rules to keep any player that was determined to stick it out, so they had to put me somewhere. They were also obliged to let every kid play, even if only for a couple of plays a game.

The plays in which I participated that stand out most in my mind were the ones where I moved before the ball was snapped which cost us a false start penalty. Then there was the time I got sandwiched between two big gorillas, got the wind knocked out of me, and had to be walked off the field. But it wasn't all bad. When we took the team picture, I got to stand next to the cutest blond cheerleader on the team! (I'm sure it didn't cause her to sweat nearly as bad as it did me.)

My response to these insecurities, I guess, contributed to my acting like a dictator toward my brothers. Some people work out to build up their muscles—I worked over my brothers to build up my self-image.

Yet, I suppose my early years were not so different than many kids—that is, until around the age of eleven or twelve. In my case, two significant changes happened. First, I learned I was adopted. My dad's cousin, Doreen, was talking to another person and commented about my being adopted. No problem, except for the fact that my brother, Mike, had overheard it.

"Mom, am I adopted too?" he asked, much to her surprise.

The cat was now out of the bag.

My memory is vague, but I seem to recall that when my parents told me I was adopted, I laughed, thinking it was a joke. Realizing they weren't kidding, my laughter quickly turned to tears. I was never to become more upset than that over the subject. I later developed a healthy attitude toward being adopted. (This was one area where a melancholy personality helped me cope with an otherwise potentially shocking bit of knowledge.) I'll admit feeling stunned initially, but what was done, was done. I simply went on with the only family I had ever known, and with minimal curiosity.

Secondly, my life changed dramatically when I went to junior high school. I was catapulted into a downward spiral that only the grace of God would later bring me out of. I was informed that I was going to Einstein, the newest junior high school, located in the newest, well-to-do part of Appleton, at the time—where kids with the newest clothes lived. Not that I was ashamed of it, but their dads weren't cops; they were business executives. I fit in like a frog on a freeway!

It felt like an evil force was behind the persons responsible for creating the district boundaries, for they seemingly conspired to draw the line down my street, forcing me to be split up from all my friends who were going to Wilson Jr. High School. We begged and pleaded, but to no avail; I was forced to go to a school where I didn't know a soul. (Another reason for my not wanting to go there, albeit a lesser one: Woodrow Wilson didn't have that embarrassingly bad hair like Albert Einstein!)

I struggled mightily to fit in. My failure wasn't due to a lack of a goal, however. I set my sights on being part of the popular crowd, the "in" crowd. For two years I bounced along the fringes of that group like a bug trying to get into a beach ball. Finally, after embarrassment, frustration, and making no friends that were worth having, I quit trying. I developed a deep seated hatred of the popular, the successful, and the rich. Instead, I found solace in "outcasts." The advertised price for entry into this group was one that I found I could afford to pay: as long as I could drink alcohol and do drugs, I was given full membership. But like a bad used car deal, I wouldn't discover the hidden cost until much later.

It all started one day when I went to visit my friend, Roger, who was a year ahead of me in school. When I got to the apartment where he lived, I was appalled to see him and another guy, Tim, drinking beer—something that was totally foreign to me. At twelve years old, I was still refreshingly naïve to worldly vices and viewed everything through rose-colored glasses where the people I knew didn't do bad things; other people did.

"You guys are drinking *beer*?" I asked incredulously.

"Yeah, so?"

"But it's . . . it's illegal!"

"Oh, just shut up and have one."

And so I did.

I don't recall having finished that can of beer, but those few sips changed the direction of my life and started me down a long, winding, drunken road.

The now infamous Roger also had the dubious honor of introducing Mr. Idealistic to the world of marijuana. One day we rode our bikes to an old, abandoned farm silo where Roger proceeded to pull out a small, fancy-looking pipe and a plastic baggy full of what appeared to be oregano. (With Roger's help I was becoming more street-smart—I had suspected we weren't going to be making spaghetti sauce!) After some cursory instruction, I took my first hit from the little pipe. Because I had asthma, one can imagine what that first inhalation was like! I just about choked to death in a fit of coughing.

"Hold it in as long as you can!" Roger encouraged.

With eyes watering, veins bulging and my face turning red, the smoke burned my eyes and lungs. It was hot and tasted like licking an ashtray. If this was supposed to be fun, it was going to take a little getting used to! But used to it I got. You might even say I became quite an expert—and even enjoyed it. I found other experts and we would all sit around, as often as we could, encircled by billowing, blue clouds of acrid smoke, cooling down our parched and burning throats with beer.

Eventually my ventures in under-age drinking and illegal drug use produced some unplanned consequences. By the age of fourteen, I had a juvenile record for drinking. As I entered my early driving years, I was pulled over twice while drunk; and another time I totaled my 1971 Dodge Monaco station wagon while drunk, sending my friend, Doug, into the windshield where he suffered a shattered jaw and facial cuts.

Incredibly, in all these incidents, I never once received a ticket for driving while intoxicated because these were the years prior to the serious crackdown on drunken driving. But that's not to say I was lucky. These events scared me but never deterred me because, by now, I was hopelessly, undeniably hooked. Had I received a greater punishment, it might have been the wake-up call I needed to produce positive changes in my lifestyle. Unfortunately, that was a long time in coming.

By the time I got to high school, my friends were, considered by most, a motley bunch. We hung out in the back of the building, just outside the commons area, smoking cigarettes (them, not me; that's one habit I never took to)—talking, listening to music, and skipping class.

One late-summer afternoon, I was sitting outside with a group of people that I didn't know very well. We were listening to a song from an old rock group called *Triumph,* and I was singing along. A guy named Ronnie, who was a drummer in a rock band, was sitting nearby and overheard me singing.

"Hey, have you ever sung in a band?" he asked me.

"No, never have."

"Well, you have a great voice, man. You want to come over and jam with us some night?"

I had never "jammed" with a band, but the flattery was enough to entice me into doing it. A week later I ended up displacing Dave as the lead singer for the five-piece, heavy metal rock band called *Alliance*. It seems the band had been looking to unload Dave for quite some time, and unfortunately for him, I happened along at just the right time.

The world of heavy metal rock music magnified my drug and alcohol use. My days were filled with eardrum-splitting band practices—as we locked ourselves away for long hours in the basement, drinking and smoking pot. Although being a lead singer gave my self-worth a much needed shot-in-the-arm, it was only temporary. By the time I was seventeen, I was in a downhill slide that led to depression. My life was going nowhere. The loneliness I felt, in spite of the "hero" status the band offered, was so acute that one day I decided to go buy some friends.

With a few bucks in my pocket, I went to the pet store and purchased a blue parakeet and a cage, a fish tank, and some fish— not great conversationalists but nice to look at! That evening, while setting up my pals in their new digs, I received a phone call from Ronnie's girlfriend, Justine.

"Hey, Edders," she replied as I answered the phone, calling me by the nickname Ronnie had given me. "You doin' anything tonight?"

"No, not really."

"Well, we're having a little party over at Paula's house with a few people and we were wondering if you want to come over."

"Uh, Okay…yeah, that's cool. I'll be over."

I didn't know Paula very well. We had met one night when my friend Tom stopped over to introduce me to her. At the time they had been going out but had since broken up. I wasn't exactly in the mood to socialize, especially now that I had a "family" to take care of, but I went anyway. It was a small gathering of about seven or eight people. Pretty tame—it was only a Tuesday night. We played pool downstairs and drank until, one by one, everybody left except me—and Paula. We played some pool and talked for a while longer. She was a real knockout at sixteen: a tall girl with streaks of golden red running through her soft brown hair—and such seductive dark brown eyes that I was afraid to stare into them for fear of going into a daze and saying something totally incoherent! A wide mouth showed off her beautiful teeth; and when she flashed her big smile, it caused her eyes to sparkle and formed deep dimples in her cheeks, making her look like a little kid. Even with that, I still thought of her only as my friend's former girlfriend.

But she sure didn't think of me that way! It's funny how you can look back on what appear to be the most insignificant events in your life and realize how they set the course for your entire future. Unknown to me, I was being pursued. The whole party was an intentional scheme cooked up by Paula and Justine to lure me over. I never saw it coming.

On this night, January 18, 1983, I was to be placed under a spell that I would be forever helpless to fight against, kissed by the girl who would eventually become my wife. They say a hummingbird's heart beats 1,400 times per minute. I had that beat, no problem! For Paula, it was a mission accomplished!

Six months later I graduated from high school with a 1.7 grade point average. Translation: a C minus/D plus. I'm still not sure if I actually graduated or they just wanted to get rid of me! It's not that I didn't have potential—had they offered classes in rolling joints or chugging beer, I might have graduated *magna cum laude*. Anyway, the future didn't look too bright, and up to this point the only notable experience on my resume was heavy metal singer, substance abuser, and near high school dropout, none of which held much hope for the future. For the next three years I worked an assortment of jobs: car washer, maintenance man, soldering machine operator, shipping and receiving clerk, swimming pool installer, and vegetable picker, just to name a few.

Paula and I had become inseparable. My family immediately loved her. I wish the same could be said about me and her family! One night early in our relationship, I went to her house to watch a movie. After I walked out the door, her step dad, Bill, said to Paula's mom, Gail, with a sour look on his face, "So is that hippy Paula's new boyfriend?" (I guess my long hair and 1960's retro-look didn't score many points with him.) Also showing concern, with a protectiveness that only an older sibling could have, was Paula's sister, Lori, who strongly advised against getting hitched up with a "heavy metal rocker."

Paula, however, was highly self-motivated and never treated setbacks as problems, only opportunities. This became a powerful example to me because I always viewed things negatively first. Since the time she was fifteen, she had a job at her grandfather's pizza business while taking advanced math classes in high school. When she was seventeen, she went to Mexico for two months at a college-level language school to continue learning Spanish. Those credits transferred back to high school, allowing her to graduate one full year early—the juxtaposition to *my* less-than-stellar high school career!

I had now lived out most of my teenage years with the subject of my adoption rarely being brought up. Not only was I fully content with the fact, but I also wouldn't have known what to do next if I had wanted to know more. Paula changed all that. She had always been intrigued about my mysterious past and could not understand my not approaching the matter with more interest. But as I was getting close to turning eighteen, she and my friend, Scott, relentlessly pressed me time and again to begin searching.

To pacify them both, I agreed to go with Scott to the Brown County courthouse in Green Bay shortly after my eighteenth birthday. I was disappointed to learn that, even though I had been born in Brown County, my adoption record was not housed there but kept by the county that the adoption was finalized in. That could only mean one other place: my home town of Appleton, the seat for Outagamie County.

There was a friendly young girl behind the counter at the clerk of courts office as we walked in. There wasn't another customer in the whole place. She smiled and asked, "How may I help you?"

"Is this the office where adoption records are kept?" I asked.

"Yes, it is."

"Well, uh, the reason I'm here is because I was adopted eighteen years ago and I am trying to locate my adoption file. I was born in Brown County but adopted in Outagamie County, and the people at the courthouse in Green Bay said that I should try here. I'm wanting to know about my birth mother."

The girl's eyes grew large causing her eyebrows to rise. She was clearly intrigued.

"Really? (She apparently didn't know—nor did I at the time—that the adoption, by law, should have stayed "closed") Wow, that's neat that you're trying to find her," she said, nodding her head. "What year were you born in?"

"Uhm…June of 1965."

"And what's your full name?"

"Edward William Herman."

"Alright….." she uttered while jotting the information down on a scrap of paper.

"We wouldn't have records from that year filed in this office. They would most likely be archived in the basement," she explained, "but if you want to wait a few minutes I can go search to see if it's there."

"Yeah, that would be great," I assured her, now starting to get excited myself.

"Just give me a few minutes. It may take a little looking to find it, okay?"

"Sure, that's fine. I can wait. Thank you."

It seemed too incredibly easy.

Scott and I waited. And waited. It was taking a long time for her to return and I was starting to feel edgy. Every tick of the clock taunted me, telling me I was crazy for doing this. Scott sensed this and even he seemed jittery, so there was minimal chitchat between us. I had ignored this topic a long time, but now I was getting uneasy about what I might learn. Whatever it would be—good, bad, or otherwise—I would be forced to live with forever. Twenty minutes later her smiling face reappeared at the counter with a red file folder in her hand.

"I've got it!" she exclaimed, beaming as if she had just

discovered the final item needed to win a scavenger hunt.

I held my breath and swallowed hard as she handed me the folder across the counter. It had the faint musty odor of old paper. I noticed a number typed on the tab: B1350.

"Why don't you sit right over there," she cheerfully offered, pointing to a small table and chair against the far wall of the office, totally oblivious to the shock I was feeling.

"Sit there as long as you want," she said breathlessly. "Oh, and would you like a pen to write with—and how about some paper?" she offered, scurrying around behind the counter, trying to scrounge up the items. I could only nod my head.

"I think I'll go walk around for a little bit," Scott suggested.

"Yeah, okay. Fine," I acknowledged absently, still staring at the file folder and gathering the pen and paper the receptionist had fetched for me. Then I was alone.

I opened file B1350. Attached to the inside cover was a legal document longer in size than the file with the lower one-third folded upwards so it would fit inside the folder. It looked like a typical legal document with blank areas for information to be filled in. Glancing at the top portion of the page that was not covered, I noticed the name *BRIAN* typed in the first blank, followed by a surname that I neither recognized nor could pronounce. Something wasn't right. *She brought me the wrong file.*

Just as I was about to go return it to the receptionist, I flipped down the folded page for one last look. The form's legalese said something about a change of name. That's when I saw it. Typed in a blank toward the bottom of the form was a name I was very familiar with: *EDWARD WILLIAM HERMAN. Amazing! Not only was this the right adoption file, but I had had a different name!*

Sufficiently recovering from that shock, I pressed onward. Not a lot could be gleaned from the rest of the file. As a matter of fact, it was rather sketchy regarding the details of the adoption and offered only perfunctory information about my biological parents. There was, notwithstanding, enough to keep my search going. My biological father was listed as being twenty-eight years old, German and Irish in descent, 5' 9" tall with a medium build, blue eyes, brown hair, and a medium-dark complexion, but his name was not listed.

I began to conjure up a picture of this stranger, now taking on distinctive features, comparing the image to my own physical characteristics. The file also recorded that he had an eighth grade education, worked as a painter, resided in Green Bay, and suggested that, not only was he not involved in the adoption proceedings, but wasn't even aware that my birth mother had been pregnant!

I was pleased to find there was more information on my birth mother. She was born on February 19, 1944 in a small town in Wisconsin, about an hour away from my home—and was of Bohemian, French, and Belgian descent (*Bohemian! My unconventional, non-conformist lifestyle was now starting to make sense—I've got Bohemian blood!*). The record also said she was twenty-one years old, 5' 4" tall with blue eyes, brown hair and a medium complexion.

I compared that to the mental picture I had created of her after I had found out I was adopted. The picture didn't match well with the description, but it didn't matter. What mattered was that the paperwork listed her name: Marilyn Anne. The phantom figure that dwelled for years in my imagination had now become a real person! Even more amazing was how I was able to find her so easily, despite the laws designed to keep me from it!

Going on the assumption that she was from the Green Bay area, Paula and I headed there a few days later to continue the search. On a whim, we checked the phone book. My hands fumbled as I turned to the "*T's*." Then they began to tremble as my finger probed down the listings and stopped on the initials, *M.A.*, listed in front of that unusual last name from my adoption record. *Incredible! It has to be her! How many people could possibly have the same initials, especially with such an odd last name?* With Paula's prodding, I decided to go all the way. Standing in a street corner phone booth, I dialed the number.

"Hello?" a woman's pleasant sounding voice greeted me.

"Hi. I'd like to speak to Marilyn, please."

"Marilyn?" she said, sounding momentarily confused. "Oh, I'm not Marilyn, I'm Marie. Marilyn would be my second cousin."

Oh, great! How am I going to get out of this without an explanation?

"I'm sorry," I apologized. "I saw the initials *M.A.* in the phone book and thought you were her."

"Oh, no, that's alright. But can I ask who this is and why you're looking for her?"

It was risky to reveal who I was to someone in Marilyn's family that might not know about me, but I decided to take the chance, desperately wanting any help she could provide.

"Well, my name is Ed Herman, and I was given up for adoption eighteen years ago," I began to explain. "I just tracked down my adoption file recently and found out that Marilyn is my birth mother."

As I told Marie the details that led me to call her, her reaction made it clear that these were not facts known beyond the immediate family, or to her. Fortunately, though, she was fascinated by the whole story and more than willing to do what she could to help me.

"I haven't talked to her in years, but the last I heard she was living in Appleton," Marie said.

She gave me the name and phone number of Marilyn's father, my biological grandfather, suggesting that he might be able to tell me where she was. It was that one tidbit of information that would lead me chillingly close to Marilyn and shake me up for years to come.

I thanked Marie for her help and asked her to please keep this conversation confidential. She hung up, assuring me that she would never bring it up to anyone in the family.

It was getting late in the day as we stood outside the phone booth, but we were so close to finding Marilyn that we didn't want to give up now. Emboldened by talking with Marie, I decided to call my biological grandfather next. Listening to the phone ring on the other end, I thought how bizarre this sleuthing was—yet it was starting to get easier, almost fun. The voice of an elderly sounding man answered and said, "Hello?"

"Yes, hi," I said tentatively, asking if he was the person I was looking for.

"Yes, I am. Who is this calling?" He inquired suspiciously.

Stating my name first, I once again launched into a brief account of who I was, just like I had done with Marie. When I finished, there was only silence on the other end.

It became uncomfortable.

"Hello?" I asked. "Are you there?"

A frail and shaky voice responded, "Yes, I'm here. What do you want from her?"

"Well, I...just...well, nothing. I just want to find her!"

Without warning, I was forced to consider what my real intent and purpose was and how it might affect others involved. The desire to know my medical history now seemed so petty in light of wrecking lives.

"I wish my wife were here; I wish my wife were here," he kept repeating, becoming agitated and starting to cry. "She knew all about you. She could help. I wasn't involved at the time."

What I didn't know was that his wife—my grandmother—had passed away a few years before.

"What do you want with Marilyn?" He demanded again.

"Sir, I'm not looking to get anything from..."

"Please, please don't call her!" he begged me. "She lives in Appleton and is married and has two sons and nobody knows about you, not even her husband!"

My stomach felt nauseous as a cold chill penetrated me, making my legs feel rubbery. Suddenly this wasn't so much fun anymore.

"Please, please don't call her! You'll ruin her life! Nobody knows!" he implored again, sounding on the verge of panic.

"I won't call her! I promise, I won't call her!" I assured, beseeching him to calm down. He finally stopped pleading and began to softly cry. Terrified that I had upset him to the point of being dangerous to his health, I tried to convince him that I was willing to let it go and not interfere in his daughter's life.

"I swear to you, I won't call her," I promised one last time.

"Please, please don't. You'll ruin her life."

Hanging up the phone, I took a few minutes to recover and get my heart rate and breathing back to normal. *If this is what this adoption thing is going to turn into, forget it! It's not worth it! Who needs to know that badly! And to think, she's married, has kids, and never told her husband about me! Unbelievable!* I now understood the need for adoption laws intended to protect the biological parents. Lives can so easily be destroyed by imprudent or insensitive adoptees.

Shook up as I was, the whole harrowing episode still continued to pique my curiosity, so I decided there was little harm in making one final inquiry. A few days later I went to the clerk of courts office back at the Outagamie County court house to research if Marilyn's marriage license had been issued in there. These, along with criminal records, birth certificates, and death certificates are public records and are available to anyone who asks to see them.

Even if I did locate her in Appleton, I had no intention of reneging on the promise I made to not contact her. I still shivered every time I thought of the call to her father.

Within minutes I had it. The marriage license showed that Marilyn had married in Appleton in 1969. A quick check of the phone book revealed her husband's name and an Appleton address—just a half mile from where I grew up! But that wasn't all: after driving by the address, I recognized it as being a house I had ridden my bike past almost every day for three years while on my way to junior high school!

For the most part, learning of my birth mother's existence and her whereabouts had little lasting effect on me. It was simply time to move on with my life.

"I need to talk to you about something," I announced to Paula one day while we ate at a fast-food restaurant.

"Okay," she said warily, unsure of why I sounded so serious.

"I'm thinking of going into the military so I can get money to go to college."

That caused her mouth to drop as if to say, *You? Rebel to the core? Yeah, right? You'll last about five minutes with someone screaming in your face!* Perhaps true, but I had become increasingly frustrated with working menial jobs and feeling like I was on a one-way road destined for "Loserdom." I knew I needed to get a degree—no matter the cost.

"If I did, would you go with me?"

"Is that a proposal?"

"Yeah, I guess it is."

"Well, then, I guess I would."

That was it. No ring, no roses, but we were engaged. I seem to recall shaking on it, then splitting a French fry.

Our plans were contingent upon me qualifying for the United States Air Force. A few months later, after meeting with a recruiter, taking a written test and passing a physical, I was now scheduled to leave for basic training in March of 1986—a lovely six week, all-expense-paid vacation to sunny San Antonio, Texas, courtesy of the U.S. Government—and we were free to plan our wedding and our future.

Our wedding day, three days after Christmas, December 28, 1985, was bright and sunny—but bitter cold. An arctic cold front had come in from Canada, following a snowstorm that had blanketed the state. My head felt like it was stuck in a bass drum during a marching band parade. The wedding party had gone out the night before to celebrate after the rehearsal dinner, but my best man and I decided it wasn't enough, so we indulged in some extracurricular celebrating until about three o'clock in the morning.

Just before the ceremony began at one o'clock in the afternoon, a few nips of *Dr. McGillicuddy's* schnapps from my brother-in-law to-be in the pastor's office helped take the edge off. I was now ready to take the plunge—especially when I saw how beautiful my bride was coming down the aisle. She could have made a small dog break a big chain!

It was a really nice wedding and a lot of people came. Even more showed up at the reception—which is normal in Wisconsin anytime there's free beer! Having exchanged our vows, we were now married. Paula had turned nineteen two weeks before, and I was twenty.

Two months later, Paula stayed in Wisconsin while I left for basic training. My flight graduated with honors. Things were really looking up. I was passionately consumed with becoming successful, wanting to prove to those preppy, stuck-up, little rich kids in junior high school—and myself—that they weren't as great as they thought themselves to be. That "I'll show 'em" attitude wasn't exactly virtuous, but at least it was driving me toward excellence.

Upon graduating I was sent to Biloxi, Mississippi again, without Paula, for Technical School to be trained for my job. Originally slated to go into firefighting, I was disqualified due to colorblindness. Given a choice of job options, I picked Administrative Specialist; that is to say, some flew jets, I flew a computer! I finished my technical school training as an honor graduate.

It was June of 1986 when we arrived at Holloman Air Force Base, New Mexico where I would be stationed for the next four years. We immediately began searching for a place to live, having driven from Wisconsin with our rental truck packed tightly, holding all our worldly possessions. Paula was excited for us to begin our new lives together. I was excited because I knew this was going to be *the* opportunity I needed to start fresh.

My initial dallies into beer and pot seemed juvenile compared with the smorgasbord of illegal drugs and hard liquor I had advanced to. The opportunities to get loaded had been endless. On two separate occasions I lived with cocaine dealers, but prior to going into the Air Force—by sheer willpower and a desire to better myself—I had managed to stop doing drugs.

We easily settled into our new life, finding a nice little place to live in Alamogordo. Paula started a job at the mall while I got acclimated to military life. Both of us quickly made new friends.

Unfortunately for me, one of my first friends was my supervisor, who liked to drink as much as I did! I had found a kindred spirit. My first weekend in New Mexico, he took me to Elephant Butte, a large man-made lake on the Rio Grande River, to go fishing. We never did put a pole in the water, and the cooler that was supposed to come back full of fish? It had left home full of beer and came back empty.

Meanwhile, I had applied to New Mexico State University and was taking classes on campus at night. It was a brutal schedule: work all day on base, race thirteen miles back home to Alamogordo, nuke a hot dog, and then fly out the door to get to my first class on time. After that, there was school for the next four hours, heading home to say, "hi" to Paula, doing homework, and then passing out from exhaustion—only to wake up to repeat the whole process again the next day!

Even though we were busy, we loved our new life, except for one remaining dark cloud—my alcohol problem. The fun we were having was continually overshadowed by my gripping addiction that seemed set on strangling the life out of our marriage. My continual drinking binges degraded into nights of blackouts, vomiting, and passing out like an adolescent novice, living through his first rights of passage into the world of alcohol.

On one occasion, Paula found me passed out with dried blood trailing from the bridge of my nose, down to my chin. Evidently I had split my nose wide-open on something while drunk and never even knew it! It got to the point that I could not plan anything without fear of doing it without drinking. The effects of alcoholism were now spreading over our lives, staining every fiber of our marriage like a spilled drink on carpet. The power I had exercised for years over the beast of alcohol had now shifted—the monster was now controlling me.

Our marriage was as good as it could be with all that drinking. Even back when we were going out for the three years prior to getting married, it was rare for us to disagree or have a fight, but now it was becoming constant. Something had to give. After an angry, drunken rage in which I had lost my temper and tried to destroy everything in the house, I, at long last, admitted to Paula that I had a problem and needed help.

The next day I went to the squadron First Sergeant and confessed my alcohol dependency. It was surprising to people around me because I had never been in trouble, never physically hurt my wife, never missed work, and was maintaining a B plus average in college. I was even being nominated on a consistent basis, and sometimes chosen, for "Airman of the Quarter" awards. The monster in me had also been a master of disguise.

For two weeks I went through intensive alcohol rehabilitation classes, anger management, and group discussion. *Here I am, a model enlisted person, on my way toward a successful career in the Air Force, in class with a bunch of drunks!* It felt absurd. Finally, after making it through the class, I resisted drinking for the next two months. What I couldn't resist, however, was feeling totally miserable without a drink.

I finally broke when a buddy came over on a Friday night while

Paula was at work. I recall thinking, because I had been doing so well, that I deserved to celebrate a little bit. Three quarters of a bottle of vodka later, I had fallen from the proverbial "wagon." When Paula came home, it broke her heart to see me having again lost the battle against alcohol.

For the next few years, I continued to fight the monster, sometimes winning for a few weeks, sometimes for only a few days. I never completely controlled "him," and always felt miserable, even if I *was* winning. It continued to take its toll on me *and* Paula.

On one of my bad nights, she came perilously close to the end of her rope.

"I will not live my whole life like this," she announced to me with steely resolve.

"Is that a threat?" I challenged.

"You can take it anyway you want to. I'm not saying that if you drink tomorrow I'm going to leave you, but I don't know how much more I can take."

I loved her more than anybody in the world. I steadfastly refused to think of our marriage in terms of falling apart. In fact, we had such a tremendous respect for our marriage, that we had an unspoken rule that the "*D*" word (Divorce) would never be uttered between us, no matter how bad it got. We were afraid of that word, believing that if we ever spoke it, we would start down a slippery slope that our relationship would not recover from.

Yet here I was, listening to the most precious person in my life tell me that she would most likely leave me if something didn't change. For the love of my wife, I had to somehow conquer the beast.

Our plan was to stay in the Air Force. Paula and I had talked it over and decided that I would reenlist when my four-year stint was up. As if to solidify our commitment to our new plan, we set our sights on a new four-wheel drive pick-up and began trying to have children.

Just before I signed the re-enlistment paperwork, something very strange happened. For reasons I could not explain, I came home from work one afternoon and announced that I had changed my mind. I was about to turn our future plans around on a dime.

"Honey, I decided I would rather get out of the Air Force, go back to Wisconsin and finish college, full-time."

"What happened?" she asked, taken aback. "Did you have a fight with your boss?"

"No. I just want to get done with college and it's taking too long doing it part-time," I replied. It was true; it *was* taking longer than I wanted but I could not have pushed any harder. Every semester I averaged only one class short of full-time status, all the while meeting the demands of military life.

I am not usually an impulsive person. Even to this day, every step I take is a well thought out, definitive plan, so this spontaneous change of direction was unlike me. But consistent with any major decision we've ever made before or since, we discussed, agreed, and planned how we would accomplish it. Paula and I had never thought we would live in the north again, but we were heading back to Wisconsin.

Unknown to us, Paula's brother Bob, the aforementioned brother-in-law who provided the wedding day schnapps, was back home on his knees diligently praying that God would somehow bring us back. (He wanted to reach out to us, but we were 1500 miles away.) Bob's life had miraculously turned around soon after we left for New Mexico. He too had been heavily involved in the drug scene and was drowning himself in alcohol every night while working as a bartender.

He would lie in bed at night and beg God to wait for him to get his life together. God heard and soon provided the answer he needed. It was shortly after praying those prayers that Bob's life would undergo a powerful change—a change he knew Paula and I desperately needed as well.

Chapter 3

January 20, 1990
Menasha, Wisconsin

*W*e arrived back in the Fox Valley area in the heart of winter and unloaded our belongings at a house across the street from the Fox River. The 10° temperature felt especially frigid because it was 70° when we left New Mexico. It wasn't only the cold air, however, that slapped me in the face when we got back to Wisconsin.

I soon learned that I had missed the registration deadline for the spring semester at University of Wisconsin-Oshkosh. The whole purpose of getting out of the service was to focus on school, and now I would have to wait until September to resume classes. Precious time was wasted because I had not thought of registering ahead of time. Not only that, but my honorable military discharge and year and one-half of college credits didn't impress any prospective employers, either. I couldn't find a job, and with hunger overtaking my ego, I ultimately ended up back at the company I left to go into the military four years prior. Instead of being in charge of operating a large piece of machinery, as I did before I left, I was hired to do building maintenance. I now took out the trash, mopped floors, and cleaned the lunchroom. So much for my plan of success!

The extreme change left me dispirited and depressed. My response to this was a familiar one: drown it! When I wasn't working, I would sit for hours on the living room floor in front of the stereo speakers with heavy metal blasting, drinking large tumblers of rum and Coke.

Paula's brother, Danny, would often stop by the house to visit.

Danny had been responsible for leading Bob to a relationship with God, and I thought he might be making me his next project. Not that I was offended by his religious talk—I always had a great relationship with Danny.

It didn't matter that I resisted; Danny was undaunted.

"Eddie, Eddie," he would say animatedly, "God can deliver you from alcoholism!"

Too bad for Danny! I'm a hopeless case! I thought. By now I was so beaten down and defeated by my addiction, I didn't know if God was real any more. I grew up being dragged to church on Sunday, but it had never meant much to me. Nevertheless, had anyone asked me if I was a Christian, I would have replied, "Yeah, sure, I believe in God!"

As a matter of fact, I had what I would consider a divine encounter about the age of twelve while watching a Dr. Jack Van Impe crusade on television one night with my mom. Something within me stirred and I began to cry. The next thing I remember, my face was buried in the carpet, and I was praying a simple little prayer that God would forgive me for my sins and come into my heart. There was no doubt He had been reaching for me that night through my repentance, but the awe of the experience would soon fade from my life.

Now I began to approach the Bible as any other book, having been immersed in the world of academia for the past three years. I was interested in what Danny showed me, not because I thought there was some supernatural revelation to be gained, but more for the appreciation of the Bible as a piece of literature. It was when he read to me certain passages of scripture that contradicted what I had always heard growing up, that I began to perk up and listen a little more closely.

"Eddie, God wants to fill you with the Holy Ghost," Danny would say. "It's the only thing that will help you overcome your desire to drink."

"Well, yeah, but I got the Spirit in me when I accepted the Lord into my heart," I replied a little defensively, repeating the mantra that I had learned in church. I knew little of the Bible and certainly wasn't speaking from a position of knowledge, just my preconceived notions of the Bible.

Because of that, as much as I loved Danny and Bob, I was always a bit awkward around them because they went to a "Pentecostal" church. I couldn't explain why their church was wrong—I just felt sure it was. For years I had heard about how Pentecostals clapped, shouted, and danced around like a bunch of crazy people! And this "speaking in tongues" stuff Danny tried to explain to me was *really* weird! When I went to church as a kid it was preached that tongues was of the devil! No wonder they were so odd!

But the truth was, I was also ashamed around Danny and Bob for my two-facedness. At the same time that I became more interested in the Bible, I was also expressing to others my negative feelings toward their church and beliefs—feelings I dare not repeat in this book!

One day, Danny arrested my attention.

"Have you ever seen this?" He asked, turning to the second chapter of the book of Acts. "Let me show you what happened to people in the New Testament when they received the Holy Ghost."

Curiosity getting the better of me, I leaned in for a closer look.

"This is the account of the very first time in the history of man that God gave people the Holy Ghost. It says, *When the day of Pentecost was fully come, they were all with one accord in one place. And suddenly there came a sound from heaven as of a rushing mighty wind, and it filled all the house where they were sitting."*

Okay, what's this got to do with me? I thought.

"And there appeared unto them cloven tongues like as of fire, and it sat upon each of them and they all were filled with the Holy Ghost, and began to speak with other tongues, as the Spirit gave them utterance! Eddie, when God poured out His Spirit on people for the first time, *it* caused them to speak in an unknown language!"

I stared at the page, wondering why I had never heard *this* preached before.

Feeling slightly defensive, I asked, "So you're saying that because I haven't spoken in tongues, I don't have the Holy Ghost?"

Danny put his hand on my shoulder to show he wasn't attacking me.

"All I'm saying is that when people in the Bible received the Holy Ghost, tongues is the sign that accompanied it. It's great that you believe in God—a person *must* believe first. But God's looking to put His Spirit *in* you to help you live an overcoming life. And when that truly happens, God's Spirit will cause you to speak in an unknown language."

"And you say this experience will *deliver* me from alcoholism?" I asked, feeling so beaten down that I found it hard to believe it could be this easy.

"Yes, but not only that! Look what happens next!"

He read aloud about how those gathered in Jerusalem that day were confounded by the behavior of the 120 people that had received the Holy Ghost and began hurling accusations, saying they must be drunk. (Having much experience in the area of drunkenness, I could only imagine how they must have looked!)

The apostle Peter, Danny explained, stood up and began to tell the crowd that what they were seeing and hearing was the fulfillment of the prophesy of Joel in the Old Testament that said, one day God would *pour out His Spirit upon all flesh.* Peter then talked about how Jesus of Nazareth was the Messiah that the Old Testament prophets told would one day come, but the people had rejected Him as such. It must have been a very convincing sermon because the people were *pricked in their heart, and said unto Peter and to the rest of the apostles, Men and brethren, what shall we do?*

"Eddie, after realizing what they had done, they were really asking the question, *How can we be saved?"*

"So...what was the answer?" I asked.

Picking up at Acts chapter two, verse thirty-eight, Danny read, *Then Peter said unto them, Repent, and be baptized every one of you in the name of Jesus Christ for the remission of sins, and ye shall receive the gift of the Holy Ghost. For the promise is unto you, and to your children, and to all that are afar off, even as many as the Lord our God shall call.*

"Eddie, it goes on to say that 3000 were baptized that day in the Name of Jesus for the remission of their sins. That means that all their sins, anything they had ever done against God, were completely taken away, never to be charged against them again. Don't you see? It's a brand new start—your slate is completely wiped clean! This is exactly what you're missing!"

Hungry to discover if there were any other revelations that had been hidden from me, yet still a little skeptical, I asked, "Is there any other place in the Bible where it talks about this stuff?"

Danny assured me there were many scriptures. He turned to the tenth chapter of Acts and began to read the story of a man named Cornelius, a devout man and one who feared God with all his house. Cornelius gave much alms to the people and prayed to God always.

"Does this sound like a Christian to you?" Danny asked me.

"Yeah, I suppose he does," I had to admit.

"Okay, then. Look what happens next."

The story talked about a vision that Cornelius received of an angel. The angel instructed him to send men to fetch Peter, the apostle, so Peter could tell them words *whereby he and his entire house might be saved*. Then around the same time, the Spirit spoke to Peter and informed him that men were coming, and that he should go with them.

When Peter arrived at the household of Cornelius, he began to preach about Jesus Christ to everyone in the house. Right in the middle of his sermon it started to get interesting. Danny read, *While Peter yet spake these words, the Holy Ghost fell on all them which heard the word. And they of the circumcision which believed were astonished, as many as came with Peter, because that on the Gentiles also was poured out the gift of the Holy Ghost.*

"See Eddie, here was a believer that God knew needed something more than his belief in God to be saved! And how did Peter know that these people received the Holy Ghost?"

He continued reading, *For they heard them speak with tongues and magnify God.*

By now, Danny had my full, undivided attention.

"Watch what happens next," he went on.

Then answered Peter, can any man forbid water, that these should not be baptized, which have received the Holy Ghost as well as we? And he commanded them to be baptized in the name of the Lord.

"Do you see the pattern here? Being filled with the baptism of the Holy Ghost and being baptized in Jesus' Name is a consistent theme in the New Testament. That's why Jesus told Nicodemus in the gospel of John, chapter three, that he needed to be born of the water and born of the spirit to enter into the kingdom of God. You see, Eddie? When you're baptized in water and baptized by the Holy Ghost, you are born again!"

My stubborn and limited understanding of religious doctrine now emerged as unsupported, petty notions in the light of the Bible itself. Reading these scriptures scared me. Part of me was in awe, but the other part was afraid of the responsibility for what I now knew. A now awakened fear of God told me that ignoring the clearly written truth could not be good for my soul. Certainly I would have to reckon with this at some point, but for now it was too much to fathom. *Would I have to become one of those . . . Pentecostals?* I was doing what the Bible refers to as "counting the cost."

Paula had already started her search for God while we were still in New Mexico. My drinking drove her to seek God. Every Sunday she would attend a different church, trying to find the peace she longed for. I vividly remember one brief conversation we had.

"Do you think you would ever go to that church when we go back home?" she inquired, referring to the Pentecostal church that Danny and Bob attended.

"*No way!* I wouldn't set foot in that place!" I responded emphatically. It was final and there was no more reason to talk about it.

But now that we were home, Danny and Bob were able to share with Paula what God had done for them. Shortly after my niece, Courtney, was born, Bob, and his wife, Valerie, planned to have her dedicated to the Lord. They explained it would be a special service, what some might consider akin to a traditional infant baptism service. The only difference was that it would not be a sacrament for salvation, but simply to offer the child back to the Lord for His service, much the same way Hannah gave Samuel back to the Lord in the Old Testament. The whole family was invited to attend. I, however, chose to be busy that Sunday!

When Paula returned home, I was curious. *What did she think of it?* Paula said the service was very different than the traditional ones she was used to. The worship was exuberant, as people raised their hands in the air and prayed and worshipped out loud. The drums, piano, organ and singing were lively; and although she was a little distracted by what was going on, she could not escape the peaceful feeling welling up within her. Virtually from the start of the service, tears began to fill Paula's eyes. She was baffled by her inability to control her swelling emotions. When her mom, Gail, noticed her wiping the tears from her eyes, she explained, "Paula, that's the presence of God you are feeling."

It was the first time in her twenty-three years that Paula had experienced the tangible presence of a loving and Holy God, as He reached beyond the pain in our marriage and touched her breaking heart.

Paula never seemed the same to me after that.

I was still of the mind that if this Pentecostal stuff is good for her, great, but it's not for me! While there was certainly no denying that Bob's life had done an about-face, I just wasn't hungry enough yet to surrender my opinions. The experience Paula had at Courtney's baby dedication, however, had an impact on her—and she made it known one night that she wanted to start going to church regularly. Desperate for something to help our marriage, I said, "If you feel like it's going to help you, then that's fine if you want to go, but don't expect me to!"

She started attending church regularly, and just a few weeks later she really shocked me!

"Just to let you know, I'm getting baptized next Sunday night at church," she announced. "You're invited to come if you want to, but I'll understand and I won't be upset if you decide not to."

April 22, 1990
Fox Cities United Pentecostal Church
Menasha, Wisconsin

The day of Paula's baptism started out particularly bad for me. From the time I got up in the morning until the afternoon, I had been drinking and brooding in the living room, both heavily. At six o'clock in the evening, Bob came to pick up Paula to take her to church. Throughout the day, I had not given one iota of thought to going with her; but as they were about to go out the door, I was suddenly compelled to grab my coat. Paula's heart sank, she would later tell me, as she realized I intended to go with her. Knowing that

I had been drinking all day, she feared that I might cause a scene at church when I got a glimpse of those "Holy-Rollers," as I'd heard them called.

When I walked through the back doors of the church into the sanctuary, the first thing I saw were people praying. It was also the first thing I heard. And I mean *heard!* People were praying loudly and passionately. One woman in particular could be heard over all the others. Her earnest prayer was deep and sincere, as if she were pouring her soul out to God. It had the sound of a rhythmic melody to it. I thought, *These people must really love God to cry out the way they do.*

I had never witnessed anything like this at church before, and although I wasn't sure what to make of it, I wasn't offended. It just didn't seem right to be critical of people who sounded so genuine— unlike me, who only prayed tawdry little prayers as a last resort when I was in trouble.

After the worship service and some preaching, it was time for Paula to be baptized. Everyone crowded toward the back of the church where a large fiberglass tank filled with water sat in the corner. Bob invited me and the rest of the family to gather closer while Pastor Mark Lemke spoke a few words to my wife. As Paula ascended the small ladder placed over the side of the tank and climbed down into the water, she looked sweet and vulnerable, her white robe wet to the waist. There was a look of determination on her face, telling me the importance she placed on being baptized. She was ready for this.

A moment before Pastor Lemke was about to baptize Paula, I hugged her with a mounting jealousy because she was discovering a new peace in her life and it didn't include me. *I guess God is replacing me as the love of her life.*

Then my tears came.

If I had been drunk before, I didn't feel drunk now. I had never been one to get weepy when I was intoxicated, so I was taken aback by the emotions now raging through me. *What was happening to me?* I tried to get a grip on myself. I had an urge to go curl up in a ball on the floor and cry. *What was I feeling? Love. Yes, that was it! I was feeling love like I'd never felt before!* Suddenly there were no problems in my life, no dependency, no stress. I felt warm. I felt at peace. I too, was now feeling the presence of God Himself. At the time, I didn't understand it all, but I would soon come to realize the miracle of what just happened to me.

"Paula, upon the confession of your faith, and your repentance, and your desire to be obedient to the Word of God, I now baptize you for the remission of your sins in the Name that is above every Name," Pastor Lemke's voice boomed as he lowered her down in the water.

"In the Name of Jesus Christ!"

Right then, every person in the church that had pushed in close exploded in clapping, shouting, and praise to God. A crescendo of jubilant noise filled the air. The musicians began to sing and play and the whole church erupted in rejoicing. Paula came up out of the water with her hands lifted high in the air, worshipping God with a loud voice. She didn't even look the same—almost unrecognizable. I couldn't explain it, but something undeniable had just happened to my wife. *Has it been that long since I've seen a look of joy on her face? Has God just done a miracle in her life?*

I left church that night aware that my life was about to dramatically change. In what way, I was not sure. A few weeks later, Bob and Valerie asked Paula and me if we'd like them to teach us a twelve-lesson, in-home Bible study on Saturday mornings. Again, I was curious, but still scrutinizing scripture with the eye of an academician, approaching the Bible like a text book.

At work I had been moved from building maintenance to building security. Long, uneventful nightshifts now afforded me the opportunity to read the Bible and other Christian writings, as I searched for answers for my life. Meanwhile, as my weeks of study continued, I steadfastly prayed, along with many others, for God to deliver me from my desire to drink. What I didn't realize at the time was that He had already answered my prayer.

"So Edders, how are you doing with your drinking?" Valerie asked me while sitting around their kitchen table on a Saturday morning.

The question stopped me cold.

"Well, Val," I replied, looking down pondering, "Now that I think about it, I haven't had a drink for three weeks. As a matter of fact, I've got beer in the refrigerator at home right now, and I haven't touched it at all!"

That was April of 1990. Since then, I have not had a drink, a drop, or, more importantly, a desire for alcohol—since the day of Paula's baptism! The powerful experience I had at her baptism proved to be the miracle of God delivering me from the clutches of alcoholism!

Often I had prayed, "God, if you are real, prove it!" I tried everything I could think of to stop drinking: my own willpower, rehabilitation, love for my wife, but nothing worked. I "held God's foot to the fire," so to speak, and asked Him to prove all the scriptures that Danny showed me about how He could deliver and heal me. And now He had!

Before, I had been coming home late at night from work and drinking five or six cans of beer before going to bed. But for the past three weeks, I came home, opened the refrigerator, took out something to eat, and all the while God seemingly blinded my eyes to the beer stacked on the shelf. He erased my desire for alcohol and miraculously caused me to forget about the cupboard full of liquor bottles that enticed me to enter into another drunken stupor.

As soon as we arrived home from the Bible study, Paula and I, together, dumped every drop of liquor down the drain. There were no more hypothetical scenarios about what God might do for me; God had performed a miracle just for me! He didn't put me in a recovery program; He put the recovery program in me! I wasn't rehabilitated, I was delivered! Wholly and completely delivered! The chains that bound me were shattered to pieces, and I was liberated from the prison of addiction—set free to live like I had never lived before!

By now, I was attending church regularly, although I still didn't understand all I saw there. It helped greatly that I was learning the Word of God. I studied with diligence and hunger, compelled to find that which my soul longed for. How could I continue to deny God and His Word after what He had done for me? What Danny had told me was true. God was now tearing up my fragile notions like tissue paper in a windstorm, replacing them with the rock solid foundation of His Word. He was much bigger than I had ever imagined. I wondered what else Danny told me that might be true?

May 13, 1990
Fox Cities United Pentecostal Church
Menasha, Wisconsin

I was ready. Reflecting back, I wonder why it took so long to make the decision to be free of my past and start over anew. Ask any convict if he could have his criminal record erased and start his life completely over, what would he say? Exactly. Tonight would be my night to be baptized! But I wasn't the only one about to receive a powerful experience.

It was Mother's Day. The morning service was a special tribute to moms. But the evening service was different. Worship service started upbeat and fast with clapping and praising God. Suddenly, the presence of God fell upon the congregation; people began to dance and shout, many with tears flowing down their faces. Just like the Bible said it would happen; God was inhabiting the praises of His people!

The service turned into what's referred to in Pentecost as a "blowout." The preacher never made it to the pulpit, as praise broke out all over the sanctuary. While the musicians played on, the joy of worship burst forth so strongly that some people fell to their knees, blessing God and giving Him glory.

That's when I saw Paula touched in a special way. With her hands in the air and her mouth filled with praise, she cried out to God. I watched in amazement as her chin and lips began to quiver and shake. I was a little concerned, but not too worried—she had a look of joy on her face.

Pastor Lemke laid his hand upon Paula's forehead and prayed over her, speaking words about receiving the Holy Ghost. When he did, Paula's lips stammered, her hands shook uncontrollably, and all at once she began to speak in a language that I could not understand. People praying for her and around her began to rejoice. God was filling my wife with the baptism of the Holy Ghost just like He did in the Bible!

For forty-five minutes she worshipped. She started on one end of the altar area, praying under the influence of the Spirit, until she ended up on the other side. When Paula opened her eyes, she did a double take, surprised that she had worshipped all the way across the front of the church!

When it was over I was afraid to go to her. It was as if she'd been on a long journey and came back different. Would she still feel the same about me? Would this experience make us feel like strangers? Once she pulled herself together and wiped her face, she looked up at me, smiled, and fell into my arms. There was a new love in her life now, but Paula still remembered me. Her new love wasn't here to take her away from me, but rather to put us back together. The healing of our marriage was continuing!

The service shifted toward the back of the church where the baptismal tank was located, the same one in which Paula had parted the water only a month before. I climbed the same ladder and dropped down into the water. Rev. Jack Yonts, Sr., Valerie's father, who founded the church in his living room nearly twenty years before, happened to be in town and he was going to baptize me. Just as he was about to put me under the water, I held up my hand and stopped him. There was something urgent I had to do.

"One second, Brother Yonts," I said.

I leaned over the edge of the tank and motioned for Paula to lean in close. With my mouth next to her ear so nobody else could hear, I said, "Honey, in just a minute Jesus is going to forgive me for everything I've ever done against Him and wipe it all away," I whispered, trying to control the sobbing that was threatening to overwhelm me. "But before I do this, I have to know if *you* will forgive me for all the pain I've caused you."

She hugged me hard and began to weep.

"I do, sweetheart."

Oh, thank God! My darling, precious, and longsuffering wife, who had endured so much, had forgiven me!

Now I was ready.

Once again I heard the preacher utter those life-changing words reminiscent of what had been spoken over Paula a month ago, except they now applied to me.

"Ed, according to your repentance and your faith and obedience to the Word of God, I now baptize you for the remission of your sins," Brother Yonts intoned with authority, in a deep, resonant voice, letting me down into the water.

"In the Name of Jesus Christ!"

When I broke out of the water, my breath left me momentarily. I knew this was a spiritual cleansing, not a physical one, yet it felt as though the tangible weight of a thousand sins had been removed from my shoulders. Lifting my hands high, I thanked God for being patient and waiting for me to eventually come around. *Thank you Lord, for not giving up on me.* Unburdened, my body felt lighter. I was unsaddled of the condemnation I had carried upon my back for so long. No more would I bend under the weight of sin. The blood of Jesus now provided the answer my soul had been longing for. I was free!

June 24, 1990
Fox Cities United Pentecostal Church
Menasha, Wisconsin

People were streaming out of their pews to get to the altar area during worship service, responding to the moving of God's Spirit. Worshipers began to weep under the powerful anointing of the Holy Ghost. The slow, deep urging of the worship songs was drawing them all into His presence.

All, that is, except me. Standing in the second row by myself, I was virtually the only one left in the sanctuary not at the altar. Frustrated, I raised my hands and closed my eyes, trying to tap into what was going on. *People all around me are being blessed, so why can't I feel it, too?* Emotionally, I felt dead. *Where is the presence of God?*

By now I had attended church long enough to experience many blowout services—and this night appeared to be no exception. It looked like the preacher would have to save his sermon for another time—God had something else in mind!

With my eyes closed, I didn't realize that Bob had joined me until he spoke. He laid his hand on my shoulder and began to pray in a soft, melodic tone. The words shot straight to my heart. They began to melt the wall of ice surrounding my soul. It was *exactly* what I needed to hear! As that wall melted, tears welled in my eyes, overflowing and cascading down my face. I shuddered as the unencumbered presence of God now cloaked me.

My head dropped and my knees buckled. A pressure was building deep within me like a raging river. The dam was about to burst. When I finally released that last vestige of the old life that I'd been hanging onto, the Holy Ghost came like a flood. Suddenly I blurted out words I didn't understand, yielding to the rush of living water that sought to spring forth within me. Now I knew for sure. It was for me! It was for *me*!

For years I craved the euphoria brought on by drugs and alcohol. I drank, inhaled, ingested, sniffed, and snorted anything I could to kill the pain of not liking myself, seeking to check out of life long enough to feel some peace. But never, ever, had I experienced anything like this! I had been buzzed in almost every way possible, but never had I encountered a high like the one I now felt! Peace. Joy.

Finally, I understood why scripture calls it *joy unspeakable and full of glory*! It leaves you speechless—there are just no words to describe it. God had miraculously filled me with the baptism of the Holy Ghost! *Praise God!*

After that, the restoration of our marriage was profound. People at church that had only known us for a short time often asked us how long we had been married, assuming we were newlyweds. By repenting over our sins, being baptized in His Name, and being filled with His Spirit, God made Paula and me new creatures in Christ. Like the Bible says, *old things are passed away, behold, all things become new.* Our relationship toward each other blossomed as we grew in our relationship with God.

We couldn't be involved enough in the kingdom of God. Six months later, we were helping our youth pastor, Jack Yonts II (currently my senior pastor), in youth ministry. Six months after that, I was leading worship services with the voice that had once cursed and defiled God through heavy metal rock music. Filled with the Holy Ghost and compassion, we put our hand to the plow and reached out to anybody who would listen to our testimony of how God had changed our lives.

In a few semesters I would be graduating from college with a Bachelor of Science degree in criminal justice. The urge to start a family came back to Paula and me at the same time. But along with that desire, however, came the nagging question of my medical and genetic background. *Was there anything to be concerned about in my biological history? Should we forget about it, or was it too risky to ignore the unknown?*

Inevitably, the subject of Marilyn came up. *Do we dare attempt to contact her?* It had now been about seven years since I spoke to her father, and just the thought of that conversation still sent a shiver up my spine. *Please don't call her. Nobody knows. You'll ruin her life!*

After much prayer and discussion, we decided it was worth the risk, but only on two conditions: one, Paula would make the phone call. The shock to Marilyn might be too much if I were the one to call, not to mention the fact that I was scared to death after what happened last time. Secondly, I told Paula that if it didn't go well, she was to promise Marilyn that we would never call again. The last thing I wanted was for her to be looking over her shoulder for the rest of her life, wondering if and when we would suddenly pop up. I rationalized it was the one small way to assuage the guilt I was going to feel for going back on my promise to her father. I could only hope and pray that his prophesy about ruining her life would not come to pass!

Emotionally, I tried to prepare myself for two possibilities. Either she would be elated to finally have an opportunity to meet me, saying, "I'm so glad you found me. I've often wondered about you throughout the years," or, that she would say, "I'm sorry, but I made the decision to give you up a long time ago. I'm glad your life is good but I'm not interested in meeting you."

"Do you want to be with me when I call?" Paula asked.

"No way," I said adamantly. "I'll wait downstairs, here."

Paula smiled, kissed me lightly and started up the steps to the office. I paced anxiously across the living room floor, palms sweating and stomach rolling, thinking, "There's no way to prepare for something like this." A few seconds later I heard Paula shout down to me.

"It's ringing!"

Chapter 4

February 19, 1944
Algoma, Wisconsin

*M*arilyn was the first of three children, growing up on a dairy farm in southern Door County, Wisconsin. They were difficult times for a young family in America. World War II had been raging on for three years in two major theaters: Europe and the South Pacific. The thrust of "Operation Overlord" which would ultimately change the course of the war in Europe would not happen for another four months. Allied troops were preparing to storm Normandy's beaches, plunging headlong into the teeth of Nazi resistance. They dug into the coastline of France, thereby beginning the arduous task of gradually breaking the back of Hitler's aggression. Back home on the small farm, self-imposed hardships to support the war effort were the norm, but were tolerable, considering what Marilyn's family had been spared. Some had sent away loved ones who never returned.

The farm was situated almost on the county line at the southern end of the peninsula between Green Bay and Lake Michigan. Surrounded by gently sloping hills and undulating fields outlined and demarcated by patches of deciduous hardwoods and pine trees, the small house, barn, and outbuildings were far removed from the hustle and bustle of urban life.

Here, spring brought forth new leaves, wildflowers, and the need to plant, while summer ushered in the oppressive heat and humidity, helping crops to grow and encouraging the relentless assault of mosquitoes. As fall descended, it turned the leaves a brilliant montage of colors before they fell to the ground. Winter would then

come quickly, refusing to leave for months, blanketing everything in
a layer of snow—as sharp north winds from Canada sometimes
drove temperatures to below zero. In this quiet, rural community,
people were rarely found just passing through—most were related to
each other in some way. And those that weren't knew all the others
by name.

Marilyn's parents—my grandparents—grew up as neighbors and
eventually married in 1942—in the same Catholic church, a few
miles down the road from the farm, that the family would faithfully
attend every Sunday. They were private people; and although they
had a few close friends, their social circle was small and limited
mostly to family. It was hard to get Marilyn's father to go places; he
was content to stay home and work the farm of twenty dairy cows,
and fields of corn, oats, wheat, and hay.

My grandfather came from a family of thirteen children and was
tall and thin, to which I can attribute my own physique. His shyness
made him soft-spoken and quiet. He was a hardworking, family man
whose roots could be traced back many generations to Bohemia
before it became part of Czechoslovakia.

Marilyn's Uncle Mathias (on her father's side), who was a school
teacher, undertook an extensive research project on the family
ancestry, recording generations going back farther than my great-
great-grandfather who immigrated to the United States in October of
1856. Printed circulars sent to Germany and Bohemia in the 1850's
encouraged families to come to Wisconsin stating: *The soil is
adapted to the raising of corn, rye, wheat, oats, and vegetables, all
products with which the Czech husbandman is familiar!* To this day,
with the exception of Nebraska, Wisconsin is home to more people
of Bohemian decent than anywhere else in the country.

My grandmother was also a shy, quiet woman whose mission in
life was doting on her family—having never worked outside of the
home. An extremely talented person, she sewed every stitch of
clothing the children wore (until they were of an age that they could
rebel, in favor of store-bought wares!) When she wasn't helping
with the farm chores, she could be found in the kitchen, cooking for
a growing family. She also loved tending to the flower garden, but
most of all, her creativity was unleashed in photography. It has taken

many scrapbooks to hold all of her black and white photographs taken over the years, some having won awards.

Marilyn was much like her parents: shy and soft spoken as a child. Above all else, she would become the "girl" in the family. Marilyn wasn't in love with farm life and didn't particularly care for the backbreaking and sometimes messy chores that it required. A person was more apt to find her hunkered down somewhere in the house with a book in her hands. She was an intelligent child who did well in school, and for a time, took piano lessons, although she never became passionate about it.

When Marilyn was two, her brother, Steve, came along. Finally! A son to help with the manual farm labor! Steve took after his father in personality and physical traits. He also was quiet and soft-spoken. (This personality trait seems so prominent within the gene pool that I often wonder how I missed out on it!) Like his dad, Steve loved to be outdoors helping to keep the farm running smoothly.

Another two years went by and another daughter came along. Carol was the tomboy of the family—the absolute antithesis of her older sister. While Marilyn was always clean, dressed nicely, and played in the house, Carol roamed outdoors, usually ending up in the barn, getting dirty. Growing up, they shared a bedroom where Marilyn's side of the room was plastered with pictures of Ricky Nelson.

Life on the farm was wholesome for the close-knit family. Most weekends, especially during the summer, the farm was overrun by children. Friends, neighbors, and cousins would come to play. Many times they would spend a week or two at a time out at the farm to romp in the fields, play in the barn, and climb the silo—an endeavor that always resulted in a scolding from Marilyn's mother.

Marilyn's cousin, Jim, tells of a "favorite" game where the kids would follow the dairy cows around the pasture and wait for one to deposit a cow pie. Once they found a cow that complied, all the barefoot kids—including lady-like Marilyn—would step into the warm, steamy manure, squishing it between their toes!

Dozens of pictures show the children as they were growing up. Marilyn's mother was continuously dressing up the kids in different outfits and costumes, then positioning them in various poses in an attempt to produce the perfect picture. The three children, as well as a multitude of cousins and neighbors, immediately knew it was picture time when the broom stick came out. Marilyn's mother used it to measure the distance from camera to subject. The children understood rule number one: you never posed farther than the length of the broom stick!

All Marilyn knew as a child was a peaceful and safe childhood where honest, good-hearted, church-going folks loved their families as well as their neighbors.

Not long after graduating from high school, however, Marilyn's life drastically changed. She moved to Green Bay to work, sharing an apartment with a friend. When she was nineteen years old, her roommate advertised an item for sale in the paper, and a man responding to the ad came to the apartment. He was seven years older than Marilyn, with a worldliness about him that she had never been exposed to before. He was a little scary, yet fascinating.

Still shy and reserved around people, Marilyn was immediately captivated by him, flattered by the interest he showed in her and not in her roommate—whom Marilyn considered much prettier and more outgoing. Being around him was like standing in line for a roller coaster ride when you have an innate fear of speed and heights—she was both scared and thrilled at the same time!

A relationship began, but it didn't last long. From the beginning, Marilyn's reservations about him were confirmed. He drank heavily and often which usually led to violent behavior. Soon after meeting him she learned of his prison record; but by that time she felt trapped in a bad situation—not only fearful, but terrified. When she was finally able to escape the relationship, her shame and embarrassment about it kept her from confiding in anyone—especially when she discovered she was pregnant.

It was 1964 and strict cultural norms were in place. Having a baby out of wedlock was unacceptable. You were either a good girl or a bad girl. So Marilyn resisted telling anyone who she desperately wanted to protect from embarrassment. Remaining silent also protected her from having to explain a regrettable relationship—a subject she wanted to completely forget.

As she began to show evidence of her pregnancy, Marilyn borrowed a tent dress from her sister, Carol. Fortunately, they were the fashion trend of the time, formless and baggy, able to hide the signs of the growing life within her. She would only gain twelve pounds during her pregnancy, enough to make some wonder, but not enough to substantiate their suspicions.

As the time approached for her to give birth, Marilyn cashed in an insurance policy for $1000 to pay for the hospital expenses she would incur. Then she contacted Catholic Social Services and went through a series of interviews with a case worker to begin the process of putting her baby up for adoption. She was eventually required to go through a hearing which would forever terminate her parental rights.

On June 8, 1965, Marilyn gave birth to a boy, the first in a series of miracles. Why a miracle? Because there were other alternatives available to her that she chose to ignore. Marilyn endured the whole ordeal alone, saddled with the terrible memory of how she found herself in this spot.

Marilyn remained silent, pressing and stuffing her thoughts, emotions, and memories of what had happened deeper into the dark recesses of her heart and mind. On the outside, she lived an apparently normal life, but she felt forever changed on the inside.

It wasn't until her mother inadvertently came across some misplaced insurance paperwork that anybody in her immediate family knew.

"Did you have a baby?" her mother quietly asked one day when they were alone.

"Yes." Marilyn replied, simply.

Although her father, brother and sister would eventually come to know about it, not another word of the incident would be mentioned in the family until many years later.

Almost three years later, she was living in Appleton when she met a man in the piano bar area of George's Restaurant, a popular social hangout at the time. He was much older than she was; twenty-three years older, in fact. But Danny's humor and good natured personality were hard to resist—and a relationship began.

If it's true what's said about opposites, that they attract—then such was the case with Marilyn and Danny. For as much as Marilyn was a quiet, shy, introvert, Danny was a complete extrovert. He was a small man, only slightly over five feet tall, with a barrel chest and a big, welcoming smile that never left his face. The size of the man may have been small but the size of his laugh was not. His booming laugh was delightful to listen to and put a smile on people's faces whether they were part of the conversation or not. He was quick with one-liners and always had a joke ready for every occasion.

Danny was known by people everywhere. His large social circle was a very important part of his life. At one point, before meeting Marilyn, he landed a job with Eastern Airlines in Chicago: a dream job that required him to work with people—a talent right up his alley. He worked the job for a year, then quit and moved back to small-town Appleton because he got frustrated with walking into places where nobody knew him!

On March 8, 1969, Marilyn and Danny were married. A little over a year later they had their first child—a son, whom they called Joe. Four years after Joe was born, they had another son whom they named David.

Like the home Marilyn grew up in, her own family was close-knit. They spent time together; and as the children grew, they developed traditions, most of them revolving around sports. Danny loved sports and had many connections in the sports world, including friendships with the Appleton Foxes minor league baseball team. Joe and David were privileged to hang out in the locker room, getting to know the players (some of who went on to have spectacular major league careers.)

Danny also had close friends who had luxury box seats at Lambeau Field, so Sundays were spent in Green Bay rooting for the Packers. During the 1970's, Marilyn was a die-hard fan (commendable, considering they were some of the leanest years in the history of the team). Joe remembers her standing to her feet, clapping her hands together, and shouting, "Hotdog!" whenever Green Bay would score a touchdown. So rare was a Packer touchdown back then, that her exuberance probably caused every zealous hotdog vendor in the stadium to immediately descend upon her section!

Danny also served for many years as the chairman of a local

sports banquet that was held annually in Appleton. It brought in some very high profile athletes and people affiliated with a myriad of sports. Every year the family joined in the ritual of preparation to make it a successful evening.

Another family tradition was Tuesday "Men's Day," when Danny would take the boys around town with him to pay bills. It included lunch and numerous stops along the way to chat with the dozens of people Danny knew. David learned that his dad would become engrossed in conversations and forget to introduce him, so he eventually compensated by offering his hand to whomever they were talking to, introducing himself.

There were also family vacations every year; Europe, Canada, and the eastern and western United States, not to mention the weeklong summer getaways to the grandparent's dairy farm for the kids. Joe, in particular, loved the farm as a child. When it was eventually sold, he cried inconsolably while looking out the back window of the car as they drove away from the farm for the last time.

David and Marilyn had a special relationship. Many nights they could be found in the kitchen cooking together, listening to folk music on *National Public Radio*, or simply talking about intellectual subjects. Occasionally during the winter they would take off to a ski resort for the day, just the two of them.

Although Marilyn was raised in a staunchly Catholic family, she had not practiced her faith since the ordeal of giving up her first son for adoption. Danny was a Reformed Jew, but because there was no reformed synagogue in Appleton, he did not practice his Judaism. Marilyn could talk to the boys about spiritual issues in an intellectual manner, but the family was not devoted to any organized religion.

The combination of Christianity and Judaism in their backgrounds blended together in a way only Danny's humor could express. Every Christmas they would erect a Christmas tree in the living room which Danny dubbed as the "Hanukkah Bush." He was known for summarizing his opinion of the historic destiny of Jewish people with a sports analogy, saying, "The worst thing the Jews ever did was to put Jesus on waivers so He could be picked up by the Christians!"

Danny worked in the men's department of a large store, selling suits—a job he would work for many years. That left the primary running of the household to Marilyn. Her intellect and the perseverance she exercised in every task she tackled served her well.

For example, when Joe was in the fourth grade, she was watching television one night when a commercial came on for Tourette Syndrome. Marilyn recognized that the symptoms were similar to those Joe had exhibited as a child. She began to research Tourette Syndrome and ultimately Joe would be diagnosed at the Marshfield Clinic with a mild case of it.

Her tenacity for research gave her a wealth of knowledge that caught the attention of the Wisconsin Tourette Syndrome Association. Before long, she was giving seminars at the Marshfield Clinic and fielding questions from doctors all across Wisconsin. For the next twenty years she would help build the organization from the ground up by serving stints as President and Executive Director.

March 1991
Menasha, Wisconsin

The years flew by. The boys were growing up. It seemed that the dark secret Marilyn had buried would never be able to haunt her. Only a few in her immediate family knew, and they had remained silent throughout the years. Life was busy, but it was good. That is, until Danny was diagnosed with cancer—Multiple Myeloma— cancer of the bone marrow. It would progress slowly, but the outcome was certain. It was terminal.

Again, Marilyn fought back by immersing herself in knowledge. She thought the only way to combat the enemy was to learn as much as possible about it. She researched books and questioned the doctors, all in the attempt to fight the disease. Danny fought it too— with the humor and positive outlook which he was known for.

Marilyn took complete charge of the situation by doling out medications, making doctor appointments, and asking all the questions. It was a difficult time for her, and the heavy burden and stress dominated her emotions for the next couple of years.

Then the burden got unexpectedly worse with the untimely phone call that jerked her past back into the present.

"Hello?"

"Hi. Is this Marilyn?"

"Yes?"

Hoping to confirm without a doubt that this was the right person, Paula gave Marilyn the two names that Marie had told me years ago, and asked if these were her parents.

"Yes," Marilyn said cautiously, now becoming suspicious. "Who is this please?" she asked.

"I'm calling about Brian, who was born June 8, 1965," Paula paused for a moment. "My husband is adopted and we believe that you are his birth mother."

Marilyn's heart sank. *It was a closed adoption! Nobody was supposed to be able to find me—ever! Thank goodness nobody is home right now! How did they find out? How do I stop this?*

"How did you find this information?" Marilyn quietly demanded. Panic seized her, fearful that her whole past (which she believed to be long forgotten), would now start to unravel and be revealed to her husband and children who knew nothing about it.

"Through his adoption file and public records at the courthouse," Paula explained.

"I'm sorry, I can't help you and I don't know what you are talking about."

Taken aback by this unexpected response, Paula scrambled with what tactic to take next.

"Are you saying you're not her?"

"I'm saying, I can't help you and I don't know what you're talking about," Marilyn quickly replied, sounding as anxious as Paula about what to say next.

We had been so sure we had the right woman, but it was now quite obvious to Paula that Marilyn didn't want to acknowledge that fact to us. Also painfully clear was that, more than likely, this would be the first and last opportunity to communicate with her. Hoping to put her at ease and woo Marilyn into conceding who she was, Paula began to tell her about me. If nothing else, Marilyn would hang up with the knowledge that her child's life was going well.

"You know, some birth mothers wait their whole lives for their child to contact them because they want to know about them," she said invitingly, "and by chance that that's the case here, we wanted to contact you."

Attempting to appeal to her motherhood, Paula persisted, "We are getting ready to start a family and were hoping to find out his medical history."

"I'm sorry, I can't help you."

Marilyn wasn't budging.

"If I could just tell you a few things," Paula carefully persisted, "We have been married for six years and dated for three years before that. We lived in New Mexico for four years while my husband was in the Air Force where he won a lot of awards."

Paula didn't pause for a breath between sentences so as not to allow Marilyn a chance to interrupt and prematurely bring an end to the call.

"Right now he's finishing up college which he started when he was in the military. Things are really going great and he's had a good life to this point."

Listening to Paula confirmed one thing for Marilyn: she had made the right decision to give her child up for adoption—my life seemed to be going reasonably well. She let Paula ramble on, terrified that if she stopped her, it might make her mad. *No telling how much they might persist then! They have the advantage. They know who I am, but I still don't know who they are!* Marilyn understood undoubtedly that we were in control.

"I'm really sorry, but I just can't help you," she pressed one more time, hoping it would convince the woman to give up her inquiry.

After a few seconds of silence, Paula finally acquiesced.

"Well . . . thank you for your time, anyway," she said politely, but dejectedly, before hanging up the phone . . .

Marilyn's letter to her friend, Lori—

...one morning the phone rang. A woman asked for me by my maiden name and I said that was who I was. She wanted to talk about "Brian," and, although I didn't consciously know my son's name, I knew immediately who she was talking about. She was his wife and she wanted to tell me about him.

Lori, it was my worst nightmare come true, and at the worst possible time. Danny was sick, and you, more than anyone else, know how much that affected me. David was going through a severe depression and I was so worried about him. Other things were happening, none of them good, and now this!!!! I did what I realize now was unforgivable. I denied that I was the person she was looking for. I denied that I had had a son and that her husband was that child. I did listen to her talk about him, telling me that he had had a good life and was doing well. But right to the end of the conversation, I denied that it was my son she was talking about.

I didn't know what to do, Lori. I didn't know what they would do. I could imagine them showing up on my doorstep, or even calling again and having Danny answer the phone, or Joe or David. I was afraid. Not just about having everyone find out about him, but because I was still seeing his father's face when I pictured him. I was SURE that he had his father's face.

I even thought about calling a lawyer to see if there was anything I could do, but I didn't even know his name, only the name "Brian."

That call did one good thing for me, though. I had convinced myself all along that my son had been raised by a good family and that I had done the right thing when he was born. I made the right decision. His wife's call confirmed that for me. Now I didn't just KNOW it was true, I had proof, through his wife's words.

Eventually the acute fear faded when nothing more happened, but it was always in the back of my mind. The original terror was still there, too, that black part of my life that I couldn't bear to look at, the fear from decades earlier…

Chapter 5

*H*aving prepared myself for one of two outcomes, neither of which took place, I wasn't sure how to feel after Paula conveyed the conversation she just had with my birth mother. But as the night wore on, I felt increasingly more hurt and rejected. *How can Marilyn possibly ignore the fact that she is my birth mother? She's the one!* Before the call, I was afraid to expect anything, good or bad, but this left so much unresolved. *And to think, she's only five miles away on the other side of town!*

I had been content to live for years without knowing anything about my background, but now, after coming so close to answers, my heart ached with a desire to know how I came to be. It seemed a cruel fate to be this close, only to have it end in absurdity, like a tie game in baseball—no winner, no loser—just fans left speculating on the better team. I guess her father was right; she was so desperate to not have the hidden secrets of her life turn her world upside down that she did the only thing she could think of at the moment—she denied me.

For days I wrestled with knowing I was denied. It was hard not to take it personally. My pastor at the time, Mark Lemke, became a real blessing to me. We counseled together and his wisdom and willing ear helped me to come to grips with this difficult event. In the end, my comfort came from a scripture found in Romans which says, *For ye have not received the spirit of bondage again to fear; but ye have received the Spirit of adoption, whereby we cry, Abba, Father. The Spirit itself beareth witness with our spirit, that we are the children of God...*

Yes, I might have felt the sting of denial by my birth mother, but not by God. When I received His Spirit, as the scripture says, I was adopted into *His* kingdom and God became my heavenly Father. I had the unique experience of being adopted twice, and now I was an heir to the King of kings! Regardless of my earthly heritage, I now clung to a heavenly promise!

By January of 1993, I had a diploma and a six-month-old baby. Jordan was born in July, just before my last semester of college started. *What a blessing!* Even though I had actually had a strange dream that our baby would be born with red hair, we were still shocked by it. Even the nurse was surprised. As he was being born, she said, "Well, I don't know what it is yet, but its definitely got red hair!" I'll never forget the miracle of my first child being born. Only a parent can appreciate the awe and wonder of the experience.

After graduation, I took a job with a local company as a sales representative selling construction materials to contractors. It was a relief to be done with school, but now I was busier than ever, working a job and serving at church in many different roles.

God was continuing to bless us in so many ways. Financially, He was providing for us. It didn't seem like we were making a lot of money at the time, but we always had more than enough to live on. He was showing us that only in God's economy can you do more with less.

At the same time across town, Danny continued working through his illness. Everyday he went into the store with his trademark grin and sold suits. Marilyn continued to manage his sickness, making sure he didn't forget his medication. As the years passed, and he became increasingly weaker, she drove him to his doctor appointments. The street they lived on was undergoing major road reconstruction at the time, and there were many bumps, holes, and uneven surfaces along the way. If driven over, they would cause Danny tremendous pain. Marilyn had lovingly mapped out a meandering path through the construction zone that was smooth and flat and spared him the jarring pain.

About two years after Jordan was born, I had been home from work for about an hour and was just finishing up the newspaper when Paula and her mom, Gail, came in the front door.

"Guess who's in the paper again?" I asked, as they entered the kitchen.

Suspecting the answer, Paula retrieved the newspaper which was opened to the sports section. Danny's picture was imbedded in the article. It was reporting the annual sports banquet being held in downtown Appleton. After serving over twenty years as chairman, this would be Danny's final year. His health was beginning to deteriorate to the point that he didn't have the energy to continue working.

"Let's go!" Gail exclaimed, a devious little smile forming at the corners of her mouth. "I'll even buy the tickets!"

Paula turned to me. "Ed, do *you* want to go?" she asked, uncertain of my reaction to the idea.

"No, that's okay."

What seemed like a clever opportunity to see Marilyn up close, scared me. I envisioned showing up at the banquet and immediately shocking Marilyn because I looked exactly like my two half-brothers, or worse yet, like my biological father. No, it just wasn't worth taking that chance. Besides, all it could produce was more frustration for me. I would finally see her in person and then not be able to talk to her because I knew how she felt about my being revealed to her family.

"Well . . . do you mind if I go?" Paula asked.

I could tell she really wanted to—but was willing to give up on the idea if there was even the slightest hesitation on my part. We both knew this wasn't a game.

"No, it's alright. You go ahead."

"Are you sure you don't mind?"

"It's fine. Just be careful, alright?"

A week later, Paula and Gail were off to hear racecar driver, Mario Andretti, give his speech at the banquet—and to see my birth mother! As they entered the hotel, there was a man standing behind the information table giving directions.

"Go around this corner to the right," he said, pointing, "and there will be a woman behind the counter named "Marilyn" who will give you your tickets."

"Marilyn?" Paula blurted out.

"Oh, do you know her?" the man said, his interest piqued.

Caught momentarily off guard, Paula stammered, "Well...uh, I don't *know* her, but I know *of* her."

Whew! That was close! she thought.

Having gathered her wits, Paula proceeded around the corner of the lobby. When she got to the counter, there she was, a woman who looked older than the fifty-one years Paula knew Marilyn to be. She was heavy-set, with permed, gray hair and large glasses.

"Hi, can I help you?" Marilyn offered.

"I'm here to pick up my tickets. My name is Paula Herman."

As Marilyn retrieved the tickets, Paula stood by, amazed by the irony. Here she was only a few feet away from Marilyn, and eight months pregnant with our second son. *I'm standing in front of her, pregnant with her grandchild—her own flesh and blood!* Paula's mind raged, as she struggled to appear just like any attendee.

Marilyn handed the tickets over the counter.

"Thank you, very much," Paula said and left to go be seated.

When they entered the banquet hall, Paula and Gail were seated at a large round table for eight and patiently waited for the events to begin. Minutes later, Marilyn and her family came in and were seated—fifteen feet away at the next table! From where Paula was seated, she faced them directly.

For the next two hours, she watched, unnoticed, as Marilyn's family interacted. Paula noted that Marilyn's sons and I resembled each other. The oldest, Joe, resembled me the most. He had the same dark brown hair, blue eyes, and distinct nose.

It was obvious to Paula that Danny was very sick. When they honored him for his years as chairman, he had to be helped up to the podium. Paula's heart went out to the family—it appeared he might not be with them much longer.

One month after the banquet, our second child, Jonathan, was born.

Two years passed. It was autumn in Wisconsin, and the Green Bay Packers were hosting the Detroit Lions at Lambeau Field on a crisp, early November day. Danny and Marilyn were in their friend's skybox seats. Just as Detroit scored a touchdown, Danny collapsed. Even in his weakened condition, when he came around a few moments later, he urgently scanned the field and asked, "What happened?"—referring to the game. He would be a sport enthusiast right to the end. The next day in the hospital the doctors were not very encouraged. The prognosis was that he wouldn't make it through the day.

David, who was living in Milwaukee at the time, drove up to Appleton. He, Joe and Marilyn stayed with Danny throughout the day until Joe and David insisted that she go home for a bit to get refreshed. It had been a long day.

As the evening wore on and Marilyn returned, it was obvious that Danny was slipping away. Around ten o'clock in the evening, they gathered next to him on his bed to say their goodbyes. When he finally breathed his last breath, he passed on, surrounded by the three people in the world who loved him the most.

The next day when I saw his obituary in the newspaper and the article in the sports section that honored him, my heart ached for my birth mother in her time of loss.

Another two years passed without much talk of my birth mother between Paula and me— her name rarely came up. It was shortly after Thanksgiving when Pastor Yonts and I scheduled lunch together at our favorite BBQ pit to catch up with each other. During our talk, he brought up his daughter, Lily, who was less than a year old. She had been adopted by him and his wife, and Pastor Yonts wanted to get my perspective on how she might someday feel about being adopted.

"Listen Bro, if you're okay with it, I would like to ask you about your being adopted," He asked me.

"No, no problem. I'm an open book," I said. "I'm fine with all of that and it wouldn't bother me a bit to talk about it. I'd be glad to help."

Pastor Yonts asked me how I felt when I first learned of being adopted, how old I was at the time, and what I thought was the right age to tell a child. I answered candidly, careful to remind him that my feelings and experiences could vary dramatically from Lily's once she got older.

One thing I had learned from meeting many adopted people is that every person handles it in a different way. Some are driven to know and cannot rest until they have uncovered all the answers of their heritage. Then some like me are curious, yet satisfied if they never learn the truth. But even with that attitude, I reminded him, the denial I received from the first phone call with Marilyn still rocked me for a few days afterward.

"You know, I have only one regret about Paula calling Marilyn seven years ago. I never had Paula give her my name and information," I said. "That way, if she ever decided to change her mind about meeting me, she could look me up on her own terms."

"Do you ever think you'll try contacting her again?"

"Well, now that you mention it, her husband passed away exactly two years ago, this month," I explained, "and I've often thought that once some time had passed and she had the opportunity to grieve, *maybe* I would have Paula try one more time . . .

Marilyn's e-mail to her friend, Lori, written on November 29, 1999 . . . one day before receiving Paula's phone call—

Dear Lori,
I love autumn. It's my favorite season, always has been. I love the way it looks and smells and sounds. Danny died in autumn, so my life changed forever in autumn and even that seemed appropriate. Autumn became sort of a "taking stock of my life" time for me.

It had now been about eight years since Paula made the phone call to Marilyn. Much had changed for all of us. Marilyn had lost her husband of twenty-seven years to cancer, and by contrast, we had brought two children into the world. The topic of my adoption was rarely brought up in the house. As a matter of fact, we never referred to Marilyn by name, always as my birth mother. It's not that we purposely avoided the issue; it just wasn't part of our every day lives. The only time it came up was when people would look at Jordan, then look at us, and proceed to ask the same question, "Where did he get the red hair?" Like pressing "play" on a tape recorder, we would launch into our prerecorded answer: "Well, Ed is adopted . . ." And so it would go. Although I was thinking about contacting Marilyn again, I never thought to say anything to Paula about my lunchtime conversation with Pastor Yonts earlier in the week.

The morning of November 30th I was gone on an appointment, Jordan was at school, and Paula and Jonathan were home. The inspiration came to Paula around ten o'clock while she was down in the den exercising.

Call Marilyn.

It was a strong and evocative voice. *That's weird,* she thought, *why would I think of that? We haven't talked about her in a long time.*

At first, she ignored the voice speaking to her and continued exercising.

Call Marilyn.

Paula stopped. She looked up at the ceiling and spoke aloud, "God, is that you? Am I really supposed to do this?" The impression was so strong, it was impossible to ignore.

"Well, God, I sure hope it's you because I'm going to go do it!"

Without any forethought of what she would say, Paula went upstairs, looked up Marilyn's phone number, and proceeded to dial.

"Hello?"

"Hi, is this Marilyn?"

"Yes, it is."

"My name is Paula Herman and I spoke to you many years ago. My husband is adopted."

There was an audible sharp intake of breath heard through the phone line as Marilyn realized what the call was about. She let it out slowly.

"The last time I spoke to you, we forgot to give you our information," Paula explained, "and I would like to give it to you now, if you want it."

There was only silence on the other end.

"If you would like to meet, my husband would love to meet you. If you don't, he's fine with that too," Paula went on say. "We'd also be willing to send pictures, if you wanted them. But we want you to know that the ball is in your court, and you don't ever have to worry about us showing up on your doorstep, sending letters, or calling you ever again—if you don't want us to."

The silence continued as Marilyn muffled the sound of her crying which had begun as soon as Paula started speaking.

"If I could say anything, it would be to say that you would be very proud of him. He's a wonderful man, a wonderful husband, and a wonderful father. We have two boys. They're four and seven."

Paula hesitated.

"Would you like information on how to contact us?"

Marilyn felt from the moment she knew the purpose of the call that her life was about to change. *This is it,* she thought. *Our meeting is inevitable.*

"Yes, I would," she answered quietly, her emotions still making it hard to speak.

Paula felt stunned but elated, fighting to maintain her poise. *She's not denying him this time! She's really going to give this a chance! We might actually meet her!*

"So, what would you like? Name, address, phone number?" Paula asked, a bit unsteadily.

"Well, just give it all to me," Marilyn requested.

After Marilyn had written it down, Paula ended with one last comment.

"If Ed could say anything to you, it would be to say "thank you" for doing what you did," Paula said, perchance this might be the last time they talk. "You had other options, yet you chose to give him life."

Both of them started to cry unabashedly.

"And I would like to thank you too," Paula said.

They hung up without any strings attached.

Marilyn's letter to her friend, Lori—

...at 10:30 on the morning of Tuesday, November 30, the phone rang and my life changed forever. A woman told me her name was Paula Herman and said that she had talked to me about her husband several years earlier. I thought it was a Tourette Syndrome call until she told me he was adopted. And again, I knew instantly who she was talking about.

But Lori, this time, for some miraculous reason, it was different. For the first time, that terrifying face didn't appear in my mind's eye and I could listen to her without that fear that had covered over any thought of my son. She knew I was her husband's birth mother and I didn't deny it. I didn't ask questions, I just listened, and cried.

She told me he was a wonderful husband and father. She told me a little about his life. She told me about their two children. She offered to send me pictures if I wanted them. She told me that if I knew about him, I'd be proud of him.

She said that he had no regrets or resentment toward me. She told me that I had nothing to fear from them. She said that the reason she was calling, was because their phone call years earlier was intended to be the ONLY phone call to me, and if I didn't want anything to do with them, that would be the end of it.

But they realized later that she had never told me his name or how to get in touch with him if I ever wanted to. So THIS call was intended to give me that information, and ONLY that. She said they would never call again. Now it was up to me to do whatever I wanted to with the information. She was so gentle and sensitive. She said everything right.

I wrote down the name and address and phone number that she gave me and when I hung up, I cried some more. But, this time, there wasn't any fear in it. Not even the thought of embarrassment or shame. And I knew what I was going to do. I think I knew, all the while she was talking, what I was going to do...

Just after noon that day, I came home. Paula had eaten lunch, then turned off the ringer on the phone so any incoming calls would not wake Jonathan, who was napping.

"Honey, I did something and I hope you're okay with it," Paula said.

What did you buy now? I thought, a sly little grin forming on my face. Knowing how frugal she was with the household funds, adhering to a tight budget and not free-spirited when it came to spending, I was more amused than concerned with the thought of what she might have done without consulting me.

"What did you do?" I asked her, as if she were a naughty little girl.

"I called Marilyn."

The grin immediately disappeared.

"And?" I asked, tilting my head forward, my eyebrows raised in surprise.

I became increasingly more astounded with every detail as Paula recounted the events of the day. My stomach churned and my legs felt rubbery. I couldn't believe I was hearing this.

"So, where do you think it's going to go from here?" I queried, once she was finished.

Afraid to speculate, Paula answered, "I don't know. I'm just glad that final phone call is done. No matter what happens, we don't have to ever worry about it again."

By this time, I had seen the hand of God in many situations in our lives and in the lives of others. I had no doubt that God could perform miracles. He brought us back home to Wisconsin to find salvation. He delivered me from the addiction of alcohol. *But, what was He up to now?*

Later that afternoon, when Jonathan was awake and Jordan had come home from school, we were down in the den playing together. Paula was walking through the kitchen and noticed the message light blinking on the phone. Evidently she had forgotten to turn the ringer back on and never heard the phone. She checked the caller I.D. before listening to the message. It was *her*.

"Ed!" she called down the stairs. "She called and left a message! Do you want to come up and listen to it with me?"

Man, what an emotional rollercoaster this is getting to be! I was back to being nerve-wracked again about my adoption. I jokingly thought about the "good old days" when my life was so much easier—plain, dull and relatively boring!

"No, I don't think so," I said, as I drew back into my comfort zone.

Marilyn's letter to her friend, Lori—

...twice during the day I called back, but no one answered and I didn't wait for the answering machine to pick up. I was afraid that the voice on the machine would be his and I wasn't ready for that. I only wanted to talk to her. Then late in the afternoon I tried one more time, and let the machine pick up. I'm glad it was her voice. I left a message asking her to call me back. And quite soon she did.

"Marilyn, this is Paula Herman. I'm returning your call."

Marilyn began speaking without delay. "You mentioned in our earlier conversation that you'd be willing to send pictures," she said.

"Yes," Paula confirmed.

"Could you send a photo of all four of you together?"

"Sure, I can do that."

"I would also be willing to receive any letters you would like to send."

"Okay," Paula said, pleased that Marilyn seemed more at ease with her.

"I would also like to apologize for that phone call years ago—for what I said and how I treated you. There were circumstances in my life that are no longer there."

Although that previous conversation had left Paula feeling hopeless and disappointed, she didn't expect an apology or explanation from Marilyn. She appreciated it nonetheless. She was also fairly certain that Marilyn was referring to her husband, Danny, when she said this.

"Maybe someday this can go beyond photos and letters, but I can't promise you anything," she concluded.

"Okay, that's fine." Paula reassured her.

Marilyn's letter to her friend, Lori—

> *...this time I did all the talking and, of course, still more crying. I asked her to send me pictures of the four of them. I told her that if they would like to write to me, I would like to read anything they had to tell me. And then I told her that I wanted to apologize to her for what I had said to her during our phone call years earlier, for denying who I was. I explained to her that there had been things in my life then, that were no longer there today, and that maybe this time it could be different, but I couldn't promise that yet...*

The next day I began working on what I called *The Resume of a Lifetime*. I wanted so badly for my first letter to Marilyn to accurately depict my life and my family, briefly and concisely. It took me many hours over the course of the next week to complete the five page letter. It needed to be sincere but compelling—it might be my only chance to connect with her . . .

Ed's first letter to Marilyn . . . four days before our first meeting—

Dear Marilyn,

Thank you. I want those to be my first communicated words to you.

You chose to give me life some thirty-four years ago and regardless of the circumstances involved, you made a right decision. For that I honor you. I'm sure it wasn't without struggle (no decision of that magnitude is simply cut and dried). Having children myself, I can only imagine the trauma of giving up a child. So I appreciate what you did and my family appreciates it.

I hope this letter finds you and your family well. My biggest concern is that resurrecting all of this has caused you pain. I apologize if it has. I've struggled for a long time whether or not to pursue contacting you and for many years was perfectly content to let things be as they were for respect of not intruding in your life.

I had my wife promise you a few years back when she called that if you were not interested in contact that we would never bother you again. What I neglected to do, however, was provide you a way to find me, if for some reason you ever changed your mind. That has always bothered me and so I reneged on my promise and, hence, last week's phone call.

Forgive me if I've been selfish. It seems the older I get, the more I think about my history. But please let me try to put your mind at ease. I am demanding nothing from you. You owe me nothing. Not even an explanation.

You may find this hard to believe coming from someone in my position, but I don't believe an adopted person necessarily has a "right" to contact their biological parents. You fulfilled your obligation to me when you allowed me to be born. You made a tough choice many years ago, probably hoping to leave it in the past and move ahead. I just feel fortunate that you've been gracious enough to accept this letter.

However, if after reading it you decide you don't want this to go further then I will respect your wishes. If there are any conditions under which you want to continue communicating, then just name them. Likewise, if you want this to someday go beyond letters that would be fine too. So please don't think you have a "problem" now that you cannot get rid of.

I'd be less than honest if I said there weren't questions I'd love to have answers to, but you can't always have what you want and I don't want those questions answered at your expense.

So you see, you call the shots. You can have as much of this as you want or as little. If perchance this is the last communication we ever have, know that my life has been a good one up to this point. No bitter feelings about my history. No regrets.

Even though I've never met you before as an adult, you have always had a place in my heart and I will always be grateful to you for what you've done. And for that, I thank you...

[Letter continues on to describe my family and past]

Marilyn's letter to her friend, Lori—

...on the following Tuesday, I finally got the letter. The letter was from my son. His first words to me were "Thank you." He was thanking me for giving him life when I could have done otherwise. Lori, it's a wonderful letter and I think I fell in love with my son while I read it. They sent a family picture and I saw his face for the first time, but by then, it didn't matter what, or who he looked like.

His letter was as gentle and reassuring as his wife's words on the phone had been. He told me I had nothing to fear, that it was still entirely up to me to determine how far this would go, or if it would go anywhere at all. He said that if I wanted this to be our last contact, it would be.

He admitted to having some questions which he was curious about, but with no pressure for me to even let him ask them. He told me about his wife, his two sons, and himself. There were five single-spaced pages, written with intelligence, humor and above all, reassurance, gentleness and concern for my peace of mind.

Lori, I had the strangest feeling when I read that letter. It sounded familiar, as if I knew what the next line was going to say. I think what it was, was that each line said what I HOPED it was going to say. That, if I were to write a letter in the same situation, this was the letter I would try to write...

That was Tuesday, December 7. The next day I called them,

speaking to Paula again, and told them I had received the letter and considered it a gift. I told her that I knew they must have questions that I would like to answer, but that I'd like to do it in person. We arranged to meet at their house that night without their children present...

When Marilyn said she would prefer to answer our questions in person, Paula calmly responded, "Okay, that would be fine." But inside she was screaming, *YES! YES!*

I was on the road in northern Wisconsin when she called me later to say that Marilyn would be coming to our house at six o'clock. My plan had worked perfectly. When I wrote Marilyn the letter, I prayed that it would lead to our meeting. I also had made a subtle reference to us leaving later in the week for vacation. The last thing I wanted to happen was for her to want to set a time to meet, but have to postpone it until we got back from vacation. I couldn't bear to be gone, knowing my birth mother finally wanted to meet me and I wasn't home to do it!

It was Wednesday, the day we have our mid-week service at church. I don't miss church for too many things, but it happened to be the only night we could get together with Marilyn before leaving. I called Pastor Yonts and explained our dilemma. He understood and graciously relieved me of my duties for the service.

Once I got home, the arrangements had been made and there was nothing left to do but get things cleaned up—us and the house! *Oh, what a night this is going to be! God, give me the right words to say. Anoint me with the Holy Ghost that my light shines and Marilyn sees something different in me!*

Standing on the edge of a monumental time in my life, no matter the outcome, I had a feeling I would never be the same after tonight!

Chapter 6

December 8, 1999
Menasha, Wisconsin

*M*arilyn left the house at nine o'clock that night. It had been an emotionally draining evening and my throat was sore from talking so much. Long-awaited answers to my questions cascaded like a waterfall. I was tired, but exhilarated by the whole affair.

Paula and I were confident that the relationship would not end with this night. So many barriers had been taken down, allowing all three of us to draw closer. By the end of the three hours, Marilyn and I had developed camaraderie, standing together against all that was unpleasant about our shared past. It affected us both in different ways, yet we were now allies. Paula and I left for vacation two days after we met Marilyn with a peace of mind, knowing that when we returned, she wanted to be part of our lives in the future.

Sure enough, two letters were waiting for us in the mailbox when we came home ten days later . . .

Marilyn's letter to Paula and Ed—

Dear Paula and Ed,

I came home last night a different person than the one who drove away earlier, with her heart pounding and her hands shaking. What happened last night changed my life, pure and simple. Something like that doesn't happen every day.

No matter where this relationship ultimately goes, no matter how it plays out, I want you to know that your sensitivity, your thoughtfulness, your gentleness toward me last night, and in our previous conversations, Paula, and in your letter, Ed, will stay with me forever.

Paula, I want you to know this—that even though Ed is the connection tying us together, you're as important to me as he is for two reasons. First, I have to say again that were it not for you and the words you spoke, this incredible thing might never have happened. And, secondly, I see you and Ed as a single entity, two people so close together that I can't think of one without the other.

Ed, I wish I could think of something profound to say just to you, but when I think of you today, my thoughts are in a whirl. The only clear picture I have in my mind is of your face. What I was most afraid of turns out to be beautiful and already familiar. I think of you and the future with eagerness and anticipation.

I can't quite bring myself to write those three words to you to tell you how I'm beginning to feel about you, not because I don't feel them, but because it's so much, so soon. Just know that someday, when I CAN say them to you, I hope I can hear you say the same words back to me.

Marilyn

Marilyn's letter to Ed—

Dear Ed,

I'm writing to you to explain something that I've been thinking about more and more—actually, ever since Paula's phone call last week. It's a subject we touched on on Wednesday and one that I don't think I was clear about, mostly because I still hadn't figured it out myself.

I want to tell you about my feelings toward you during the first thirty-four years of your existence. To sum it up . . . I didn't think about you. And the reason I didn't think about you is that I couldn't think about you without thinking of the other person first. He had such lasting power and influence on my life that his memory covered over everything else in my mind.

To try to think about you meant having to reach down and push aside memories much more powerful and painful and frightening than the idea of "you." Like touching a hot stove, I learned to stop the pain of it by not touching it anymore.

So I convinced myself because it simply HAD to be this way in my mind that you were okay, that I had done the right thing when you were born. I never once questioned any decisions I had made about you because that would have meant going back to touch the hot stove. I put my faith in the agency that took care of you.

My memories from that time are so foggy (they always have been) but an overriding feeling I've always had from that time is that I was treated compassionately by the people who helped me/us. That made it easier to convince myself that you really were okay.

Can you imagine my relief when Paula told me years ago that it was true? Now I didn't just "know" it, I had proof from Paula.

I told you that on some level I did think about you as you were growing up. But I can't make it a pretty picture by saying that I thought each June of you as a baby, a young child, a teenager, a young man and as an adult, and wondered how you were, wondered about the details of your life or was curious about you. I still wasn't thinking about "you." There was still the fear and pain that never lessened and covered over "you."

But one thing I want you to know is this; the fear and pain didn't come <u>from</u> you. I would still have felt every bit of it even if you had never existed. So, the thought of "you" isn't what caused me pain, it was the thought of "him." Do you understand what I'm saying?

I'm not saying I wouldn't have made the same decision about your future if "he" had been someone else. I tried to explain that to you, too. It was the times I was living in, the family I was a part of, other factors that made that decision necessary. I know my thoughts of you over the past thirty-four years would have been different, though.

I don't know why, but on the morning of November 30, 1999, everything changed...and from that moment on everything did change, <u>even before I heard what Paula had to tell me or received your letter or saw your face</u>. That point is important because I don't want you to think that all of this has happened because you turned out to be someone I found acceptable. It would have happened no matter who you might have been or the kind of person you had turned out to be.

The painful memories are still there, but they're off to the side somewhere. To feel the pain of them, I have to go looking for them

and I don't see any reason to do that. Now the first thought that comes into my mind is of "you."
   Marilyn

We immediately called to thank her for the wonderful letters. They were a tremendous blessing to come home to.

While we were away, Marilyn's friend, Daniel, had traveled from South Carolina to visit her. Years ago, she met Daniel on-line in the Tourette Syndrome chat room. They became fast friends and subsequently met in person at a conference in Washington D.C. Suffering from Tourette Syndrome, Daniel became an unfailing friend and confidant to Marilyn.

In her, he found an invaluable love and friendship as equals although she was twenty-five years his senior. She needed his ability to listen now more than ever. For years she had suppressed her past, unable to share it with a single soul. Now she was ready to burst.

Daniel would be the first person to hear the story of her hidden past in its entirety.

Two nights later we had dinner at Marilyn's house with Daniel. She reassured us how important it was for her to meet the kids, but asked if we could get together without them one more time.

It was a toss-up as to what was better that evening: Daniel's culinary talent in the kitchen or his sense of humor. Either way, we had a terrific meal and a great time laughing and getting to know each other. After dinner, Daniel thoughtfully disappeared down the hall to watch television in the bedroom, allowing the three of us to continue building our relationship in private.

While Daniel was in the other room, Marilyn said, "Now, just to let you know, I *do* want to meet the boys," she assured us. "How are you going to explain me to them?" she asked.

"I would prefer to tell them the truth, if that's alright with you," I said.

"Do you think they'll understand?"

"I think so. Our pastor and his wife just adopted a little girl and they understand that, so I think they'll be alright with it."

"Well, what do you want them to call me?" she asked, "I'm not comfortable with the 'grandma' thing."

"How about *Marilyn?*"

"*That* I'm okay with."

Before we went too far with our relationship with Marilyn, Paula and I decided we better start telling our families about her. We invited my Mom and Dad over for dinner two nights after meeting Daniel. When we were almost finished eating, the moment felt right to break the news.

"Mom, Dad," I said nervously. "There's something I need to tell you about."

"Okay. Is everything alright?" they asked, concerned.

"Yeah, everything's fine," I assured them.

They waited for me to go on.

"Um… two weeks ago, I met my birth mother, Marilyn."

They stopped chewing—their silverware halting in mid-air—staring at me with unblinking eyes, waiting.

"Paula called her and she came over to our house to meet us on December 8th."

I brought them up to date on how it all happened. They listened, with Dad making most of the comments as Mom brought her emotions under control. He said they always thought this day might come, they understood my curiosity, and they supported me in my decision to contact her.

"I'd like to meet her," Mom said after I finished the story. "I would like to thank her."

Paula said, "That's great because Marilyn said she would like to meet anybody that we want her to."

The stage was set for my parents to meet my birth mother.

We didn't see Marilyn or Daniel for the next couple of weeks as they traveled over the Christmas holiday, but we planned to have dinner again at Marilyn's shortly after New Year's Day—this time with the boys. It was a smashing success! Again, the food was outstanding, but the highlight of the night, by far, was Marilyn meeting Jordan and Jonathan.

The first words out of Jonathan's mouth to her were, "Can I spend the night?" The kids immediately bonded with Daniel. He is a kid at heart, and Jordan and Jonathan found a kindred spirit in him.

Two days later Marilyn e-mailed Paula to say what a great time she and Daniel had with the boys. She wrote, "We've decided they're the most beautiful, talented, well-behaved children in the world."

We could not have agreed more.

Paula and I weren't the only ones with the burden of telling family what was new in our lives. Marilyn had scheduled time to talk with Joe and David, who were living in Door County where they were partners in a roofing company. She told them it was very important and she needed their full attention.

Marilyn had friends who owned a house in Door County. It was set on a small bay along the Lake Michigan shoreline and had a smaller guesthouse on the adjacent property where Marilyn would stay when she came up. Her friends rarely used the guesthouse, and over the years had offered it to Danny and Marilyn to use for their family get-aways.

The three of them planned to meet that night at the house the boys rented about ten miles away on the other side of the peninsula, so Marilyn could tell them the story their father never learned. They talked until late in the evening.

Of all they could have said in response to her amazing tale, their only concern was for their mother and the fact she had endured it alone . . .

Marilyn's e-mail to her friend, Daniel—

This morning I went to where Joe and David were working to pick up Beatnik [David's dog], and I had another conversation with them. They said they had stayed up until 2:00 AM talking about what I had told them and reading Ed's letter to me.

They were even more accepting this morning and eager to meet their new brother and his family. I'll tell you again, they have not one bit of resentment or regret that I told you—before I told them. They understand why that happened and are even happy that you were here for me when I needed you most.

Daniel, as I've said many times, if I had written this story as I hoped it would happen, I wouldn't have written it as it DID happen

*because it's all too good to be true. And this morning with my
conversation with Joe and David, the goodness continues. How lucky
can one person be?*
    All my love, Marilyn

As the depth of my relationship with Marilyn slowly grew, the
awkwardness and tentativeness of our conversations lessened. Paula
and Marilyn, by contrast, were like hand-in-glove with each other.
Of course they had no genetic baggage to wade through like the two
of us did. Still, it was getting easier for me and Marilyn to be
ourselves around each other and not become so tongue-tied.

Fearful that we were still making that important first impression,
we measured every word and opinion, not wanting to damage the
esteem we sought to build in the other one's eyes. Our mutual
hesitancy to move too fast—lest we somehow jinx this fairy tale—
resulted in us taking great care in guarding certain areas of our lives
that we weren't ready to disclose yet.

One of those areas for Marilyn was her health. She was forthright
about the medical history on her side of the family, but was tacit
concerning her present health. The only time we uncovered tidbits of
what she was struggling with was when it was impossible for her to
keep them from us.

Marilyn's e-mail to her friend, Daniel—

*I just got back from the doctor. They tested my blood sugar again,
and there's no mistake. It's high again, so it really is diabetes.*

*Daniel, I still can't believe this is happening to me. Suddenly I'm
high maintenance; I've NEVER been a high maintenance kind of
person.*

*I HATE this!!!!! I hate everything about it!!!!! There aren't words to
tell you how much I hate this. I hate seeing the pill bottles and
monitors sitting on my kitchen counter!!! I hate the list of doctors'
appointments!!!!!! I hate having to keep track every day of what's
happening. I hate it!!!!! I hate it!!!!! I hate it!!!!!*

*I'll do what I need to do, the monitoring, taking the medications,
the diet, the exercise, because I know I have to, but I don't think I'll
ever be comfortable with it. And I sure don't relish the thought of*

having to tell my family, which I also know I must do, giving them another worry, not just about me, but about their own families, too...

Having Marilyn in our lives made for a busy schedule. Running to and fro, it seemed like we were having dinner at someone's house every night of the week. They were all important occasions, especially because it usually meant one of us was meeting someone new.

One such occasion was the night we met Joe and David. I had been nervous the night I met Marilyn, but it was tempered by the thrill and adventure of the unknown. This was different. I was petrified. These were my biological half-brothers and we shared a common parent. Never had I been able to say that about anybody, ever, and the anticipation practically made me sick to my stomach.

Entering Marilyn's house, it was obvious that everybody was anxious. We shook hands all around as Marilyn made the introductions. Everyone tried hard not to stare at each other. I found Joe and David to be very polite and courteous.

As soon as the pleasantries were over, Marilyn lined us up along the wall for pictures, in birth order, no less.

"Paula, come here! Come here!" she said, frantically waving her hands for Paula to come. "Well, what do you think?"

This was the second time in as many months that I felt like a zoo exhibit! I was having flashbacks of the night I met Marilyn when she scrutinized me so closely. They compared features; eyes, hair, and noses. We continued to pose for obligatory family photos, none of us particularly excited about the camera being invited to dinner.

Before dinner I instinctively searched for common ground on which to strike up a conversation with my new-found brothers. Someone mentioned golf. *Bingo!*

"So, do you guys play?" I asked.

"Yes. We get out on occasion," Joe said, while David nodded his head. "How about you?"

"Yes, I play a lot for business and occasionally for pleasure."

We bantered back and forth about the golf courses we'd played—and spoke modestly of our handicaps. In my excitement to make a good impression, I told them about a course I was very fortunate to have played recently.

"Have you heard about the new course in Kohler called *Whistling Straits*?" I said.

"Yes, I think I have," Joe answered.

"Well, I just played it a month ago and it's awesome! One hundred and sixty bucks a round, and that's not including tipping the caddie," I boasted. "See, you have to use a caddie. And the clubhouse is *so* opulent, you wouldn't believe it! They clean your clubs for you and . . ."

On and on I went, not realizing until I was too far along, that I sounded like a pompous fool. *Oh yeah, you big, high-stakes businessman, aren't you something special!* The story didn't come out sounding the way I intended, nervous rambling that it was.

I fretted for days afterward, hoping they didn't go away from our first meeting thinking I was some arrogant nincompoop. Besides, I've since golfed with Joe; and as awesome as he plays, I've decided to quit the game!

In keeping with our plan to meet all significant family members on each side as quickly as possible (and thereby perhaps breaking a new *Guinness* record for the most new family members fed in one month), we continued to schedule dinner parties.

The next one was at my house so Marilyn could meet my Mom and Dad. My parents had already arrived by the time Marilyn got there. They hugged each other when introduced. My Mom had tears in her eyes, and as she pulled away from Marilyn, she looked her in the eye and said earnestly, "I just want to thank you. You've given us the chance to be blessed for all these years."

Dinner went well. At first, there was a subtle tension in the room as everyone tried to get to know each other, but eventually we all relaxed and conversation flowed easily. After Mom and Dad left a couple of hours later, Marilyn stayed for a post-meeting assessment.

We all agreed it went quite well, and it looked as if Marilyn would even be having lunch with my Mom in the future. Neither of my parents had appeared threatened. By the same token, Marilyn felt accepted and appreciated by them. It was important to me that no one misunderstood my intentions by thinking I was attempting to replace the mom who raised me.

Marilyn's letter to Martha and Don—

Dear Martha and Don,

Today was another highlight in a whole series of highlights over the past two months. Meeting the two of you was so very special and something I had been waiting for.

I imagine that mother/child reunions aren't so rare, but I can't imagine that many have been as happy and wonderful as this one has been. And the reason it's been so wonderful for me is because you and your family have made it that way.

Ed and Paula have made me feel so comfortable every step of the way. They've never pushed me or asked anything of me that I wasn't prepared to give. Their understanding and acceptance of me and what I had to tell them has been heartwarming.

And the same is true of both of you. Your acceptance of me today, your graciousness, made it a day I'll always remember. I feel that I made two new friends today and that this connection we have will only become stronger.

Martha, you thanked me for giving you my child, and I thank both of you for sharing him with me now. I thank you, too, for confirming what I had always hoped was true, that he was being raised by parents who loved him and were giving him a good home.

I look forward eagerly to seeing you again, getting better acquainted, and learning more about Ed's life as only you, his parents, can tell me.

With love and my eternal gratitude, Marilyn

The beauty of this evolving relationship could be seen in what it meant to each person. Jordan and Jonathan gained another grandmother, Marilyn gained another son and a daughter-in-law, Paula gained a best friend, and I gained someone that *Webster's Dictionary* has no word to describe. To call her "birth mother" sounded too practical; to call her a friend, ignored the power of our biological connection. Yet, I didn't feel at liberty to call her *mom,* out of respect for the woman who raised me. There was simply no word to adequately describe who Marilyn was and what she was quickly coming to mean to me.

Marilyn's e-mails illustrated the point that she had, to say the least, become slightly preoccupied with her new family . . .

Marilyn's e-mail to her friend, Daniel—

Daniel, sorry, but I seem to be obsessing on this new family of mine. I can't seem to think about much else. So, here's your daily e-mail, and it's about them, again.

This is my response to a note Paula wrote. Gail is her mother, who I've met and like very much. She and Ed are very close. She's been concerned that someone is going to get hurt in all of this. Paula assures me that Gail just watches too much television. LOL...

Marilyn

Marilyn's e-mail to Paula—

Too fast?????? Gail thinks this is going too fast??????? You want me to tell you if I feel it's too much, too fast?????????? Paula dear, please tell Gail, and I'm telling you, it's more like not fast enough!!

On the days when I see you, or talk to you, or hear from any of the four of you, I relive it over and over. On the days when I don't, I miss you so much. I miss the hugs. Ed's big strong ones that bring tears to my eyes, Paula's that tell me she loves me, and Jordan's and Jonathan's, making myself stop hugging before I really want to so I don't scare them away. I miss all your eyes: the blue ones that pull me in and make me forget everything else, the beautiful brown ones that see and understand everything, and the whatever-that-beautiful-color-is ones that simply take my breath away. I miss your smiles, the sounds of your voices.

I love walking into your house and your coming into mine. My heart beats faster when I hear your voices on the phone. I love looking at my calendar and seeing your names written there. I love knowing that I've brought something into your lives that you find of value. I love knowing that the people around us have accepted and embraced us and this experience.

So, no, it isn't too fast or too much and you aren't ever going to scare me away.

Yes, Paula, I agree we're beyond the superficial and in a little deeper now, and I welcome that. On the other hand, I don't want to dig into places that are off-limits. So, please tell me if I'm the one who's asking for too much, too fast. I don't ever want to scare any of you away, either.

I love you, each of you individually, and all of you together...

All my love, Marilyn

Paula's e-mail to Marilyn—

Dear Marilyn,

Here is the way I feel about you in words. I know it might be mushy, but it is true.

YOU are classy and elegant, but yet not intimidating.

YOU are sweet, loving and caring, but don't beat around the bush.

YOU have such a SPECIAL way with words!!

YOU know just WHAT to say, WHEN to say it and HOW to say it.

YOU are truthful and honest.

YOU are independent, strong, yet soft and tender.

I'm sure I could keep going, but I think you get the picture<grin>. If ever you have a stressful or trying day and just want to say hi to the kids (or even us) you are welcome to call us. There doesn't have to be a specific reason to call. You are special to all of us and we all love to hear your voice.

I Love You, Paula

Paula's e-mail had made Marilyn's day and provoked this response:

Marilyn's e-mail to Paula—

Tongue-tied again.

Paula, I got your note this morning and promptly started to cry. Then I printed out a copy to take with me to work [at a tax preparer's office]. I'll sneak peeks all day.

You lovely, precious girl. Thank you for another gift. I love you.

Marilyn

Marilyn's e-mail to her friend, Daniel—

You left one month ago today...
    Today's e-mail is about my new family . . . again. I got a call last night from Jordan telling me about the new addition to the family, a parakeet named Sugar. The kids are so excited about it! Jordan told me all the "technical" details about him and then Jonathan got on the phone. Talking to him makes me laugh and cry at the same time...
    ...I love you, dear friend. Hope all is as well as can be.
    *kiss (((((((((HUGS))))))))))
    Marilyn
P.S. So, I was just wondering, would Sugar be my great grandbird? *wink

Marilyn might have feigned confusion about her new place in our lives, but it was Jonathan that *really* needed some greater comprehension . . .

Paula's e-mail to Marilyn—

    ...Jon and I went shopping for a new picture for above my buffet in my dining room. I wanted to ask him a few questions about you to see if he really got it. I asked him "What is Marilyn to Dad?" He said, "She is his birth mother." I asked him if he knew what that meant. He said "No." Then I asked him who had him in her tummy like I had him in my tummy? He said, "Marilyn." So far so good right? Then I proceeded to explain to him how you gave birth to daddy just like I gave birth to Jordan and him. He said in astonishment, "YOU MEAN I'M ADOPTED TOO?"...

Paula and I prayed that God would continue to allow us to find favor with Marilyn. Clearly she enjoyed getting to know us, but we wanted to make sure we didn't push on her the "God stuff," as she called it. We all loved being together, but did Marilyn's desire to take part in our lives include *all* functions? We weren't sure. Eventually, there would be a family event that had something to do with church. Then what would her response be? It didn't take too long to find out.

Ed and Marilyn

*Paula, Marilyn and Ed having dinner at Marilyn's house
a few weeks after meeting.*

*Jordan, Marilyn and Jonathan (with Beatnik and Daisy)
at the guesthouse in Door County.*

*Jordan at the guesthouse in
Door County.*

*Jonathan at the guesthouse in
Door County.*

Marilyn feeding a goat at The Farm,
a petting zoo in Sturgeon Bay, WI.

Paula holding a three-day-old
goat at The Farm.

David and Eli

Left to right: Marilyn, Ed, Martha Herman and Don Herman (seated in front).

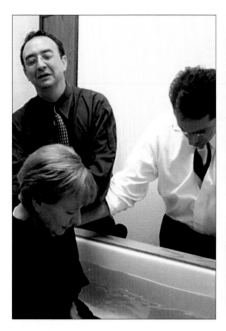

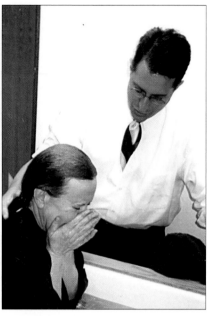

Pastor Yonts and Ed pray over
Marilyn before she was baptized.

Ed prays with Marilyn after
baptizing her in Jesus' name.

Worship service at church. Ed is on the platform leading worship;
Marilyn and Jordan are in the back row (lower right).

Marilyn setting up for a church picnic
held at a park near our house.

Nancy snaps a photo of Marilyn as she arrives at the airport in
Pennsylvania—the start of their much anticipated
vacation together (June 2002).

*Ed, Marilyn, Jordan and Jonathan seated at the
reception dinner for Joe's wedding.*

Ed teaching Bible study to Shirley.

Left to right: Ed, Shirley and Paula—Christmas Candlelight service (December 2003).

Ed, Paula, Jordan and Jonathan Herman today.

Marilyn, as her picture appears in the church directory.

"I have a question to ask you, but you don't have to answer it right away," Paula asked Marilyn while they were together at breakfast with Gail. "I was wondering *how* involved you want to be with our family. There are some family functions coming up that we would like to include you in, if you want, but I don't want you to feel obligated."

"Like what?" Marilyn said, getting right to the point.

"Jonathan's birthday party on the twelfth and Jordan's baptism on the thirteenth."

"Well . . . I've stuck my toe in the water and it's the perfect temperature, so I want to jump right in!" Marilyn replied.

Jonathan's birthday party was on a Saturday, and it was Marilyn's first time experiencing both Paula's and my family together in one place. She met a lot of people. Everyone was reluctant to take the focus away from Jonathan's fifth birthday, but it was difficult to not talk to her about coming into our lives. Careful not to spotlight her, they asked questions. It was considerate of them, especially with my Mom and Dad present. The next day, Marilyn met us at church—the day Jordan was baptized. It was her first time coming to church.

The service opened with a scripture reading. Then I led the congregation in a worship service and it was the first time Marilyn heard me sing. At first I was nervous—in particular, because I knew how she felt about religion, but also because Pentecostal worship services can be very enthusiastic and loud. She had a traditional religious background growing up which was much more subdued— and of course, one she eventually turned completely away from. It would be a unique experience for her and I wasn't sure how she would respond.

A piano and organ pumped out joyful rhythms, accompanied by a bass guitar, saxophone, drums, and singing. People worshipped exuberantly—clapping and lifting their hands toward heaven, shouting praises and magnifying God with their voices. Any apprehension I felt beforehand vanished as soon as the presence of God filled the sanctuary. *Oh, how I prayed that Marilyn would feel God's sweet presence!*

After worship, Pastor Yonts preached, exhorting the congregation and blessing the people with the Word of God. Toward the end of the service, Jordan came into the sanctuary from his Sunday school class and got ready to be baptized. Before being baptized, he sang a solo, accompanied by a pianist in the church. He was so cute getting into the new baptismal tank, donning his kid-size robe. He would be the first person baptized in the new sanctuary that had been built to accommodate our growing Sunday School and congregation.

With a lump in my throat, I watched Pastor baptize my oldest son. My little boy wasn't quite so little any more—he was old enough to understand why he needed to be baptized and had asked me himself if he could.

I had explained to Marilyn before the service the purpose of being baptized—and she seemed to understand. Whether or not she truly grasped the biblical concept at the time, I'm not sure, but the power of Jordan's baptism was impossible to escape. My little man came up out of the water worshipping God, with tears pouring down his sweet face.

It wasn't necessary for Marilyn to fully understand what the ceremony was about for her to see that there was something undeniably powerful in what she witnessed . . .

Marilyn's e-mail to Paula—

Dear Paula,

It's 11:30 and I hope you're sound asleep after your long, busy weekend. I enjoyed it so much and feel so honored to have been invited to Jonathan's birthday party and Jordan's baptism. Your family is lovely, Paula, and I hope I'll have an opportunity to get to know them all better. Aunt Phyllis is everything you said she was...

Thank you again for this weekend. I'm still trying to absorb it all, everything I saw and heard and the people I met. It meant more to me than you'll ever know.

Love to all my favorite groupies, Marilyn

The next week was a momentous occasion—Marilyn's birthday. Later, when she would reflect back on this evening, she would say,

"Before that, I didn't have a desire to be a grandmother." The night of her fifty-sixth birthday would change all that . . .

Marilyn's e-mail to Paula and Ed—

Good morning, my dears,
I think I'll always mark last night, February 19, 2000, as the moment when I became a grandmother. That's how much having the boys here meant to me. I heard them slip and call me "Grandma" more and more often as the night went on, so I know that's how they think of me.
We made some memories that I'll never forget, playing "Ponopoly," Jordan trying to teach me how to play, and Jonathan asking, "Do you get it now?" watching them wrestle like puppies on my living room floor, laughing and laughing and laughing, jumping on my bed like a trampoline (them, not me), and of course, the burping contest, Jordan the winner, Jonathan second, and me, a no-show. And then, the best part of the evening, snuggling on the bed, watching the movie (them, not me, all I could see was them).
Thank you for sharing my birthday, starting with the song in the morning, the anticipation all day, waiting for 6:30 to arrive, the gifts, the beautiful crystal pitcher and the boxes the boys made, the cards, to be read over and over and then kept forever, and finally, the evening that begins another chapter in my life.
I love you all so much, Marilyn

It wasn't the end of the world for Marilyn when her computer went down the next day, but it was close. One of her favorite things to do was communicating to friends and family via the computer. Through her work with the Wisconsin Tourette Syndrome Association she had met three of her closest friends: Lori, Daniel, and Nancy, on-line in a chat room through Massachusetts General Hospital. All three had become confidants and sounding boards for Marilyn's most intimate thoughts and feelings.

Sending e-mail was also an economical way for her to communicate with a myriad of other people, so when her computer crashed, Marilyn's ability to touch the most important people in her life ceased to exist. Even more frightening, was whether her multitude of saved data could be brought back safely—or would it be lost forever?

Special emergencies call for special friends. That's why I immediately recommended my best friend, Jeff, to take a look at her computer. Aside from being a genius with computers—having bailed me out innumerable times over the years—he is a godly man who selflessly gives of his time and countless talents. Without hesitation, he agreed to take on the project. Within a few days, Marilyn was back up and running—all data files safely recovered!

Marilyn's e-mail to Paula—

YIPPPPPPEEEEE!!!!!!!!!!!!! Oh, happy day!!!!!!!!!! Wahooooooooo!!!!!!!! It works!!!!!!!!!!!!! It really works!!!!!!!!!!!!!!!! I love Jeff!!!!!!!!!! I love you!!!!!!!!!! I love everybody!!!!!!!!!!!!

Thank you, thank you, thank you, thank you, thank you, thank you, thank you, thank you, thank you!!!!!!!!!!!!!!!!!!! Thank you for fixing my computer. I'll talk to you on Saturday about what to do for Jeff.

Thank you for tonight, I'll smile all night thinking about it. I loved every minute of it. I loved the dinner. I loved Sugar. I loved the wrestling in the living room. I loved snuggling with Jonathan on the sofa. I loved watching Jordan's face. I loved feeling Ed's and Jonathan's and Jordan's hair under my fingertips. I loved watching Paula across the room...I love you all so much!!!!!!!!!...

More love to you all,
Marilyn

It wasn't until I began preparations for writing this book that I realized the significance of what he did. Marilyn saved *every* important e-mail she ever wrote or received. Consequently, she was compiling a chronological record of our budding relationship, from the moment it started and beyond. Jeff didn't just save a few important files and get Marilyn back on-line, he restored the chronicle of a "miracle in the making!"

Marilyn's e-mail to Paula—

I must have turned off my computer just about the time you were sending last night's e-mail, so I didn't see it until just now.

When I read about how you're printing out my e-mails and saving them for the "Marilyn" file, my mouth dropped open and I started to laugh. You'll never guess what I did on Saturday morning, just two days ago. I re-read every single e-mail that you and I have ever exchanged!!!!!!!! I didn't print them out, but my e-mail system lets me sort messages and all of our messages to each other are in a folder called "Ed and Paula." There are 127 messages in it as of this morning. <wink>

I loved re-reading them. It was like reading a history of our lives together, reading about things we've done together, things we've talked about, and our feelings for each other.

But the "Ed and Paula" file isn't the only place in my computer where you reside. There are many, many messages to and from other people, Daniel and Lori, in particular that are all about you/us, and add to the history. There are copies of letters I've written to you and to other people that are about you. I've saved histories of hours and hours of chat with Daniel and Lori, and since January, you're in it.

When I had the problem with my computer that Jeff fixed, I have to tell you that my first thought was, "Oh no, what if I lose my 'Ed and Paula' stuff!!!!!"

So, if Ed thinks you're funny for doing what you're doing, what must he think of me???????? Does the word "obsessed" come to mind? <<<<<smile>>>>> But I don't care, this stuff is important to me, it's my whole history with my son packed into four months, every word of it meaningful and magical.

And you're right; of course, whoever writes the screenplay is going to NEED this stuff! No artistic license allowed here, the "real" story is perfect as it is...
Marilyn

Marilyn decided it was time to tell her sister, Carol, about us and her past. It turned out that the story wasn't a complete surprise to

Carol—she had learned about it many years ago from her father, but wisely and discreetly kept the "family secret."

Marilyn's e-mail to Paula—

Good morning, dearests...
   ...Well, what can I tell you about my evening with my sister? There were no surprises in it for me. I expected to hear that she knew I had a child, but neither of us know why our mother waited five years to tell her...
   I wasn't surprised that Dad told her about Ed's phone call, either. Carol and my dad had an especially close relationship which grew stronger as he got older.
   If I have one regret, it's that my parents aren't alive today to see the result of what they were so troubled about. They would see how good to me you are and how happy I am. They would love your gentle ways.
   I picture my father sitting in the chair he always sat in with Jonathan on his lap. And I picture my mother, as she always was, with her camera, taking pictures of the boys. I told Carol about Jordan and Jonathan jumping on my bed and she says that's exactly what her kids used to do at Mom and Dad's house...
   Have a good day, sweethearts...
   So much love . . . Marilyn

Discussing the past with Carol prompted Marilyn to make a request of me. *Could we go look at my adoption file together?* So much of that period of her life was either forgotten or still deeply suppressed, no doubt due to the horrible circumstances involved. Either way, she couldn't recall many of the details and this frustrated her.

I was more than willing to do it, but a snag occurred when we went to the clerk of courts office. This time, instead of an enthusiastic, young girl behind the counter willing to help me, I was told I would have to write a letter to the county circuit court judge requesting permission to view the file.

I wasn't too surprised. I had seen the file on another occasion, years after the first time. That time, I was required to meet the same judge in his office and explain that I had viewed the file previously when I was eighteen years old; and because I was so young, I only wanted to see it again to make sure I had read it thoroughly. He agreed to let me look at it again.

Like the last time I spoke with the judge, I explained that after seeing the file twice now, I had since been reunited with my birth mother and it was turning out to be a wonderful experience for both of us. He granted me permission, with one stipulation: the record would be sealed forever after that, like it should have been from the start, and this would be the last time I could ever see it again.

It seems God placed that angel behind the counter all those years ago for one reason—to gain me access to a legally sealed document, allowing the miracle to begin.

Marilyn's e-mail to Ed—

Hello, everyone . . .

Especially you, Ed. I've been thinking about you, about yesterday. I know we said we were going to put it to rest, close that chapter, but I couldn't help thinking about it. And I wondered what seeing those pages yesterday might have been like from your point of view. You were seeing those pages for the third time, but it must have been so different from the first two times when you were searching, nothing resolved, questions with no answers. This time you read those pages with the object of your search sitting next to you and at least a few of your questions answered. Did you EVER think that could happen?

All I can say is thank you, not just for arranging for us to see the file yesterday, but for finding and reading and understanding the file the first time. Thank you with all my heart. I love you, and all that comes with you. I love that you're in my life now and for the rest of our lives.

Love to all of you.
See you tonight, Marilyn

The truth was, I never would have believed I would one day be reading my adoption file along side of the woman that gave birth to me. After the traumatic phone call I had with her father, I never held much hope in ever meeting her—that is, until God got involved!

He was about to get involved again, and it would be a turning point in our relationship. I was due to go to Wausau, Wisconsin on a business trip. One of my customers was holding their annual two-day trade show. Because it was on a Friday and Saturday, we always went as a family, turning it into a weekend trip. This year, Paula had the idea of inviting Marilyn along.

We booked a two-room suite at a hotel so Marilyn could have some privacy. The night we arrived, I took us all to my favorite restaurant in the city. While we were dining, the conversation turned toward the testimony of what God had done in my and Paula's life.

"So, tell me again, exactly what happened with your marriage," Marilyn said.

"Well, it starts way back when we were down in New Mexico" I began . . .

She was intrigued by the story of what God had done for me and Paula. Our conversation was getting deep, so Paula politely excused herself and took the kids to play a video game in the foyer. Paula knew the door of spiritual opportunity was cracked and very close to being kicked wide open.

As we talked, Paula returned every so often to check how we were doing. Seeing that all was going well, she would hurry the kids away for another game. It was hard for Marilyn to believe that God had orchestrated all of the wonderful turns and twists in our lives, but she remained non-judgmental. It was undeniable that *somebody* or *something* was responsible for our radical turnaround, but she still could not bring herself to acknowledge that it was the hand of God.

After a while, I suggested we go back to the hotel, put the kids down for the night, and continue our talk. Once all was quiet, Paula, Marilyn and I sat down on her bed and continued where we left off.

"Marilyn, you have to understand one thing: I am not the one responsible for quitting drinking," I said. "It's not because I have strong character and willpower. I had tried quitting by myself and failed—many times. You know me only as the person you met a few months ago—but you didn't see the alcoholism, the drugs, and the anger I carried with me. There is only one reason we are the people we are: it's God!"

Marilyn's head dropped as she pondered that for a moment.

"Marilyn, it's not that I'm some extremely rare breed of individual. The *only* thing that gave me the ability to become what I am today is the Holy Ghost."

She glanced up.

"Tell me more about that."

For the next two hours I showed her the scriptures in the Bible that Paula's brother, Danny, had showed me many years before. I could feel the presence of God enter the room as I spoke, the hair on the back of my neck standing up. Paula's knees began to shake—something that still happens to her today when we share the gospel with people. We told her how the Bible became real to us once we understood that we could experience the same things today that are talked about in the New Testament.

We recounted our individual experiences of what it was like to be baptized in Jesus' Name for the remission of our sins—and what happened the night we each received the baptism of the Holy Ghost.

When it was over, Marilyn was speechless but her mind raced; *This is so different from what I remember of religion, yet, it's hard to argue against. There is definitely something different about them.*

It was enough to absorb for one night, especially for Marilyn. The spiritual things I told her sounded as foreign to her as the Chinese language. Nevertheless, her curiosity was the toehold I needed to begin the climb toward introducing her to the incredible, life-changing power of Jesus Christ.

Gone were the hints of reservation we all felt overshadowing us when we talked to each other. In its place was the liberty to freely discuss the God that shed His own precious blood for each one of our lives and what He wanted to do!

Marilyn's e-mail to Paula, Ed and the boys—

Good morning Ed, Paula, Jordan and Jonathan,
In the future when I think back to the days we just spent together, a lot of little moments will come to mind, moments that will make me smile, moments involving the boys and all of you.
But the memory that will loom the largest, the one I'll go back to most often, will be of conversation, REAL conversation, of being able

to ask, or say anything that's on my mind, about what's important to me/us, trusting that anything I ask or say will be taken seriously, not belittled or rejected or judged.

Paula, I wasn't really sad,—"sad" has a negative meaning to me— this was more like when something good happens, you just want it to continue. And I was tired. I didn't sleep much Friday night, not because Jon was sleeping in my bed, but because I had a lot to think about, a lot of thoughts to "replay", a lot of ideas to "test." Do you understand?

"Thank you for the weekend" sounds a little inadequate. I loved every second of it; it was comfortable, relaxing and fun. Sometimes words just aren't enough and "thank you" will have to do.

Remembering hugs, big ones, little ones, and wishing for more.

All my love, Marilyn

We were now free to take the next step—inviting Marilyn to come hear me preach. It happened a week after we got back from Wausau. I was scheduled to preach on a Sunday night, and Marilyn was thrilled to have been asked to come. She'd been to church before so she knew the order of how things went.

We had a great worship service and I was excited, this being my first time preaching in the new building, behind a new, hand-crafted pulpit. If I felt any butterflies beforehand, which of course I always did, they disappeared as soon as I approached the pulpit. I preached especially hard that night, not because Marilyn was there, but because I felt a special anointing upon me that I had prayed God would give me for this service. I wasn't looking to show off for her, but neither was I attempting to hold anything back.

I preached a message entitled, *The River That Flows*, which talked about the baptism of the Holy Ghost. The congregation was enthusiastically behind me, responding throughout the sermon with shouts of "Amen!" They also answered the call at the end of the message when I invited people to come forward to the altar.

While people prayed and worshipped at the altar, I came down off the platform heading directly to Marilyn, my shirt plastered to my body from sweat, and my hair drenched. She was standing in the pew next to Paula. She reached out to me.

"Oh no, you don't want to touch me! I'm soaking…"

She didn't care. Before I could finish warning her, she grabbed me, hugging me so tight that it momentarily squeezed the breath out of me. Marilyn grabbed the back of my sweaty head and held me for a long time. Paula noticed people watching us, trying not to stare, with smiles on their faces, and their mouths forming the words, "Awww, how sweet." There was no doubt Marilyn had never witnessed anything like this before. I can't say whether I preached a great sermon or not, but it sure left Marilyn in amazement . . .

Marilyn's e-mail to her friend, Daniel—

I've seen a lot of Ed/Paula/family lately. I told you that I was going to hear Ed preach on Sunday. Daniel, the man's a PREACHER!!!!!!! The message was lost on me, but the presentation simply blew me away. As much as I DON'T believe what he believes, I know that this is his calling in life and I have to support it. He's in his element; he's really good at it.

And he loves me. I'm more and more sure of that every day. I never doubted it, but I see our relationship becoming easier, deeper and more "personal" all the time. And I'm discovering more and more about him that just amazes me. He really is a remarkable person. I don't say that just because he's my son. That only got me close enough to be able to see who he really is. I say it because he IS remarkable in many ways.

They're all coming for brunch on Saturday to meet my niece Amy. Wish you could be here, too. I ALWAYS wish you could be here...

All my love, Marilyn

When Marilyn found out that the church recorded every sermon, she bought a large stack of blank cassettes and copied everything I ever preached. She was quick to remind us that she was only interested in listening to them to get to know me better. She listened closely to every word I used and the inflection of my voice. Sometimes she would fall asleep with her headphones on, my voice blasting in her ears. (At times I thought I've had the same effect on people in the congregation!).

It did not bother me that Marilyn was listening to my sermons only to hear me and not the message. I was convinced that eventually the novelty of hearing my voice would fade and she would begin to hear the message. After all, she would play each of them many times over, to the point that she knew my sermons better than I did! That's how I knew they were having an effect.

She would ask, "The sermon you preached called *Couch Pillows or Church Pillars*, what did you mean when you said...?" Unbeknownst to her, she was injecting the pure Word of God right into her heart.

The Bible says this of itself in Hebrews 4:12: *For the word of God is quick, and powerful, and sharper than any two-edged sword, piercing even to the dividing asunder of soul and spirit, and of the joints and marrow, and is a discerner of the thoughts and intents of the heart.* In other words, when we put the Word in our hearts and minds, it cuts through our soul and spirit and starts to reveal our thoughts and intents, laying bare the reality of who we are: sinners in need of a savior.

A person can't hear that much preaching without it affecting their heart and mind. A seed had been planted by our example, but now the Word of God was watering it, causing it to germinate and break through the hard, fallow ground of Marilyn's heart. It was only a matter of time before she would be compelled to act upon it.

Marilyn's e-mail to Paula and Ed—

And a beautiful Sunday it is! The sun is shining and I have a head full of new memories to run my mental fingers through, memories of a lovely day spent with all of you.

Paula, we need to go shopping, okay? I need to have you help me pick out some things for the boys to do and play with when they're here. I don't ever want them to be bored coming to my house. Please understand that I'm not trying to "buy" them with toys, I just want to make it interesting over here. I'd like to find some things we can do together, books, games, that sort of stuff. Will you help me, please?

Ed, I spent the evening listening to your songs and your words. Curiosity got the best of me and instead of listening to your sermons in any kind of order; I listened to "Permanent Markers" first. It was wonderful and I have some questions for you about that message which I'll save for the next time we're together.

You might think this strange, but when I hear you speak, I think of Danny. He loved to hear a good speaker. He would have recognized the drama and eloquence of the speech itself. He would have enjoyed hearing you.

Hugs and kisses to all of you. Maybe I'll see you Tuesday.

All my love, Marilyn

For a woman who previously said she wasn't interested in being referred to as *Grandma*, Marilyn was getting good at the role. Juggling a double major (Jordan and Jonathan), she was well on her way to graduating with a degree in grandparenting!

Marilyn's e-mail to Paula and Ed—

Good morning, my dears,

I didn't even straighten up the house last night after you left, Paula. I went right to bed. So I got up this morning with the place strewn with evidence of my grandchildren !!!!!! Their voices echoing in my head, voices calling me "Grandma." What a lovely way to greet the morning!!! I simply adore those little boys.

Paula, what a dear friend you've become. I love our conversations, no matter what we talk about. You're so gentle, so bright, so loving and so much fun. Everything I love in a friend and more than I ever could have expected in a daughter-in-law.

Ed, or "Marilyn's little youngster," as Jordan put it (That one will always make me laugh), I hope you made some progress last night on your message for Wednesday. I hope I can see and hear you deliver it. I'm going to work on arranging that today and I'll be disappointed if I can't be there. And I just want to tell you again this morning that I love you.

See you all very soon, I hope. Paula, I'm not nagging, but you said to remind you—don't forget to e-mail me the words to the song Ed sang Sunday night.

Hugs, kisses and all my love, Marilyn

Marilyn's e-mail to Paula and Ed—

Hello, my four darlings,

I'll be smiling all day today, reliving the weekend. It was a good one because most of it was spent with you.

I loved having the boys on Saturday night. I've discovered that I DO need grandchildren, despite what I said in my letter to Lori, but that the grandchildren I need are Jordan and Jonathan. I enjoy them and love them so much.

I loved Sunday with you. I loved the church service, watching and listening and meeting more of the wonderful people there. Thank you for lunch too, I had a great time.

And, Paula, I especially enjoyed our conversation on the phone later. It was just what I needed at that moment but somehow you knew that, didn't you? You always seem to know what I need...

All my love, Marilyn

My former pastor, Mark Lemke, used to say, *"You can learn something new everyday if you don't guard against it!"* I was about to learn a valuable lesson from Marilyn that has stuck with me ever since—the irony being that it was a spiritual lesson—an area one wouldn't think she'd be qualified in.

Marilyn's e-mail to Paula and Ed—

Sweethearts . . . all four of you,

...One more thing about your church. You say you feel good that I don't look down at you or your church. Paula and Ed, it's the exact opposite. I look UP to you and your church for what it's brought into your lives. In fact, if anything, I envy what you have in your beliefs and commitment. To believe and feel something so firmly and completely must be a wonderful thing.

I hope you're past the thought that I might see or hear something in your services that might shock me. That was never the case, and now, more and more, I see only peace and joy and love when I go there...

Kisses and hugs and all my love,
Marilyn

Marilyn's observations about our church services weren't all good, however. One night, it led to a rebuke for me.

"Why do you always apologize for the worship at your church?" Marilyn asked indignantly.

"What do you mean? I don't *apologize*," I rebutted.

"True, you don't say 'I'm sorry,' but you act like you need to explain everything to people so they're not offended instead of letting whatever happens happen," she said. "You say your worship's in the Bible and that God's presence comes when you worship. Well, then, what's the problem?"

She was right. When I thought about it, there were times I felt the need to go beyond simple encouragement and would begin to justify the hand clapping, the instruments, the praying out loud, the dancing and rejoicing. I found myself defending and validating a biblical charge that God's Word commands us to do, constrained by the ridicule of others who criticize it. But I, of all people, should know that for every person who condemns praise and worship—like I did at one time—there is another who will bless the Lord, and thereby be blessed. *To think, all this coming from a person who doesn't even believe the Bible!*

Marilyn's admonishment brought to mind a scripture in Romans that ended my instruction for the night: *For I am not ashamed of the gospel of Christ: for it is the power of God unto salvation to every one that believeth . . .*

Marilyn was right. I needed to stop "apologizing" and remember that praise and worship ushers in the power of change! Pastor Lemke was also right; you really can learn something new everyday. Especially if you don't guard against what comes from the most unexpected sources!

Thanks, Marilyn.

Marilyn's e-mail to her friend, Lori—

Paula and I had a long, long chat on the phone yesterday, something we do from time to time. I talk to her often, nearly every day, but every once in a while, it turns into a marathon conversation and we cover lots of territory, but of course, our favorite subject is Ed.

I learn so much about my son from her. She's so intelligent, sensitive, and honest, I believe that everything she tells me is the truth, so when she tells me about his feelings toward me, for instance, it simply fills me with happiness.

He loves me, Lori, that incredible man/son/friend loves ME!!!!!!!! And I don't think it's because he "has" to love me, because I'm his mother, he feels comfortable with me, enjoys my company, respects me, just plain "likes" me. Sorry, gushing, big time again. *grimace

Then later in the evening a phone call from Ed just to keep in touch. I don't actually talk to him nearly as often as I do Paula, so this was a BIG treat. (Brace yourself Lori, here comes another gusher!!) And although we didn't really talk about anything personal, except to talk a little about my trip today to tell my brother about him, the fact that it was such an "everyday" conversation, the kind any mother/son/friends would have, made it special, if that makes any sense at all.

I guess what I'm trying to say is that we (he and I) are getting easier and easier with each other, we can joke and laugh and tease and not be so concerned anymore about saying the wrong thing, we can talk about the mundane because we're interested in each other's lives and find even the mundane to be of interest.

And what I love most is that he DOES call, he DOES keep in touch, he DOES want to keep me close...I feel that I've added something of value to his life, made his life better, just as he's done for me and my life.

Telling you all of this makes me realize again how miraculous this all is, and I use the word "miraculous" deliberately. Ed and his church are big on miracles, miracles of healing, stuff like that. But I keep telling them that this is a miracle for me, the answer to a prayer I didn't realize I was praying, a prayer that everyone "prays," a prayer to ask for peace and joy in my life, and this is how it was given to me, this is the form it took...

Thanks again, Lori, for everything. (((((((((((((((Huge Hug))))))))))))) for my dear, sensitive, probably bored, patient friend. I love you.

Marilyn

Marilyn's younger brother, Steve, had been battling cancer for quite awhile but it appeared to be going into remission for the moment. Steve was a gentle, soft-spoken man much like his father and I was excited to meet him. His family lived in the city where Marilyn went to high school, close to where they grew up. We had been planning to go to the guesthouse in Door County in a couple of weeks and hoped Steve's schedule would allow him and his family to come up to meet us . . .

Marilyn's e-mail to her friend, Lori—

Dear Lori,

...I came home from an awesome afternoon with my brother and sister to your note, and it was perfect. You even put into words the answer to a question I've been asking myself—the question about "What did I do to earn such a gift?"...and your answer was that sometimes you're given a gift you didn't earn and you earn it AFTER you get it.

That's EXACTLY how I feel about this gift of my son...he's a gift I didn't earn, but now that I've been given this gift of him, I can start to earn it, and that's what I'm doing. I'm doing it when I bring "something into his life that no one else can supply," as you put it...when I love him and tell him I do...when I show him so that there's no mistaking it...what he means to me. Thank you, Lori, for putting it into words for me.

The afternoon was really awesome. It was good to see my brother looking so healthy and feeling so good. Maybe he really HAS beaten liver cancer. I didn't think that was possible.

So, I told them my story, and of all the people I've told it to, my sister-in-law is the one who cried the hardest and gave me the biggest hug. And as usual there was total acceptance of every part of the story. They'll probably meet Ed next week in Door County...

...Anyway, thanks again, Lori...for all the gifts you've given me...gifts I haven't earned, at least, not yet. ((((((((((((Hug))))))))))))))
Love, Marilyn

We had now known each other for about three months. It had been wonderful—everything was brand-new and exciting! We were riding on top of the world!

Life, though, has a way of balancing out our highs and lows . . .

Marilyn's e-mail to her friend, Lori—

Dear Lori,

I left a message on your machine this afternoon, but I might not be here when you call back, or I might not answer it.

I saw the neurologist this afternoon. I had a stroke. The CT scan was okay, but the carotid artery on the right side is 50 - 80% blocked.

The doctor was surprised I had the stroke because I've been taking an aspirin a day for months and it didn't prevent the stroke. He put me on another medication that's stronger than the aspirin, told me to do what I've been doing for the diabetes, high blood pressure and high cholesterol (diet, meds, exercise) and to come back in a year for another ultrasound. If I have more symptoms before this new med kicks in, it's surgery.

I don't know what triggered the stroke except that my blood pressure and blood sugar have been not-so-great...and there's absolutely no telling when the next one (the Big One?) will arrive.

Lovely, huh?

Lori, my mother had strokes. Two Big Ones. She survived and recovered a little from the first one, but after the second one, she was in a coma, or whatever that horrible state was, for eleven weeks. I swore that if I ever thought that could happen to me, I'd step in front of a bus. Well, it seems it could very well happen to me, and I'm still considering the bus idea. If God is really in charge, like Ed thinks He is, He's got a sadistic streak.

Lori, I'm so tired of all this. Life was just getting good. Now the fear is back and I can't stand it!!!!!!!!!!!!!!! I've got a time bomb inside of me and I can't stand it!!!!!!!!!!!!!!!!! I don't know how much more I can stand because I don't know what's coming...

My second thought was of my sons, all three of them. I've already talked to Joe and David, put them in shock again, but I haven't talked to Ed and Paula. Lori, I know this is crazy, too, but I'm afraid to tell them, what if they bail out?

I can't write any more now Lori, except to tell you that I love you and I'm sorry for dumping on you.

Marilyn

Chapter 7

April 2000
Menasha, Wisconsin

*W*e could tell something was wrong. Running at full speed all the time, I don't always slow down long enough to observe the little signs that people give off, but Paula's specialty is people, and her intuition is rarely incorrect. Nevertheless, we had only known Marilyn for about five months and we didn't know how far to extend our liberties with respect to her personal life.

"I called Marilyn earlier today and could tell something was wrong," Paula said after we got home from Wednesday night church service. "And now she wasn't at church tonight. Why don't you give her a call."

As surprising as it may seem, it was now unusual for Marilyn not to be at church. She frequently assured us that it was not for any spiritual reason, but simply to be near us, to meet our friends, and to see what we were so involved with. There was another reason too. We had started an outreach program, a contest of sorts, to see how many visitors we could get to come in the month of April. For every visitor that came to church, you accrued points. Bonus points were then awarded if the person came back again.

Marilyn decided to sandbag the contest in our favor by attending as many services as possible. When it was over we won in a landslide, but bragging rights were the last thing I cared about; she was coming to church, and like the sermon tapes she was listening to, the worship and the Word of God would eventually move her heart!

"I was worried about you. Is everything okay?" I said when she picked up. I could tell by the manner in which she answered the phone that it wasn't.

"No. I'm not alright."

"Can you tell me what's the matter?" I asked tentatively.

"I had a stroke yesterday."

Well, there it was.

"Okay," I said calmly, "tell me what happened."

It had been a mild stroke, one that she would fully recover from physically. But she was wounded mentally—her psyche shaken. Marilyn began to weep.

"Can we come over right now?"

"Yes," Marilyn said, sounding relieved.

"We'll be right there."

Paula called her Mom and she rushed right over to our house to stay with the kids. I grabbed a few things while Paula rustled up an overnight bag to take. When we walked through Marilyn's front door, nobody said a word. There was a lot of hugging while we waited for her tears to subside. We talked for a long time, read some scripture, and held each other's hand. Then I asked her permission to pray over her.

"I have seen God perform many healing miracles over the years, and I believe He can heal any damage the stroke may have caused," I encouraged. "But even more than that, I want to pray that Jesus will comfort you and give you peace about this so you can get a good night's sleep."

She nodded her head that it would be alright.

"In the Name of Jesus . . ." I began as we all held hands.

Marilyn's e-mail to her friend, Lori—

Maybe I'll see you here later, Lori, I'm not going to work today, mostly because the tears still come when I don't expect them, and I don't want to be blubbering all over somebody's tax return. The people picking up their returns this week aren't happy customers anyway.

Joe and David have been in touch this morning again, worried, of course, but hopeful and helpful. Joe spent a long time on the Net last night, he said, researching strokes, etc. He sent me a bunch of websites to check out. They're coming home on Saturday for the day so we can talk about some things.

About Ed and Paula. As it happened, Paula called in the middle of the evening about something, just a short conversation, and I still couldn't tell her. I wasn't quite ready to. But she could tell something was wrong I guess, because Ed called later and flat out asked me, so I told him the whole story.

And, of course, you were right, they didn't bail out. They both came over and stayed with me for a long time. Paula even had an overnight bag with her, thinking she should spend the night with me. And Ed brought his Bible.

Lori, what I find offensive and even repugnant, even now in every other "Christian" I've ever met, I find acceptable, interesting and even beautiful in them. I don't think it's just because of who they are and what they are to me. So I let them pray for me, and with me, and I even tried to suspend doubt and disbelief, but I didn't feel anything, absolutely nothing. It wasn't even that I felt God was out there but not showing Himself to me. I still felt, and still feel that He's nowhere. I don't think I believe in God at all.

But, on the other hand, what is it that gives Ed and Paula such peace and joy and confidence in their lives? They say it's God and I'm trying to understand that, but I'm not making any headway in their direction. In fact, every question I have raises two more questions and every doubt I have just gets dug in a little deeper as I speak them out loud.

But they're such good people, they love me and they're willing to help me in every way with no guarantee that their efforts will come to anything. Tonight I'm going to church with Ed and Paula, partly to get out of the house, partly to be with them and the kids and partly out of curiosity again.

Paula and I were thankful that the stroke was mild. Notwithstanding, it frightened Marilyn tremendously—especially because her mother had passed away from that very thing. Once she was put on medicine, Marilyn's life, for the most part, went back to normal—especially now that we were preparing to leave on a trip to Door County in a couple of weeks . . .

Jordan's e-mail to Marilyn—

FROM: JORDAN   TO: MARILYN
   I wonder what we are going to do in Dorkony? this is going to be fun, right. WOW!!!! I LOVE YOU SO MUCH!!!! Is there food at the house.
Is there snakes in the water? I hope not!
   As our friend Bugsbunny would say o, Thats all folks!!!!!!!!!!!!!!!

There was good news and bad news. The good news was that Steve and Pam were planning to join us in Door County, along with their daughter, Jamie, her husband Mike and their daughter, who was a year and a half old. Marilyn referred to her as the third cutest grandchild in the world (presumably behind Jordan and Jonathan!). The bad news, however, was that Steve's cancer had returned. This deeply bothered Marilyn, but she was determined to make this mini-family reunion a fine occasion.

We left on Wednesday, giddy about spending the next four days away from the busyness of our lives and planned to come back Saturday so we all could go to church the next day. There is nothing I could write that could more accurately describe the wonderful time we had in Door County than the following e-mail already conveys. Except to say, the moonrise lifting out of the horizon over the bay, casting its reflection across the shimmering water on that cool and crisp Friday night was one of the most spectacular sights I've ever seen . . .

Marilyn's e-mail to her friend, Daniel—

   . . .I wanted to tell you, too, about our few days in Door County. It was exactly what I needed, what we all needed, a few days together, time to talk, time NOT to talk.
   What memories we made!!!!!!! My favorite memory will be the late night conversations in front of the fire, some intense and serious, some easier. But always sitting side by side or face to face on the

sofa, sometimes holding hands, leaning forward to hug my son any time I couldn't resist it anymore.

Memories of Joe and David and Ed together, the three men in my life who seem to be becoming friends.

Memories of early morning watching the sunrise with Paula, drinking coffee with her and feeling so loved by her.

Memories of my brother and his family finally meeting their new nephew/cousin and being charmed by him.

Memories of those two little boys, their enthusiasm with everything, collecting bugs in jars, collecting shells on the beach, playing baseball on the lawn with their father, painting your Big Dipper rocks (Hope you don't mind. We can always get more.), snuggling with me in the rocking chair, sleeping with me in the downstairs front bedroom, me watching them.

Memories of Cana Island, and now other memories and pictures of my son and his family in that place.

Memories of meals enjoyed together, nothing so wonderful as those you produce, but special because of who and where we were.

Memories of the one cold, rainy day when we started the fire at 7:00 in the morning and finally let it die out at 2:00 the next morning when we couldn't keep our eyes open another minute, but still didn't really want to end the evening.

I know you realize how important that place is to me; the memories made there represent a cross-section of my life, most of the important people in my life have been there with me at one time or another and now I have my newest memories to run my mental fingertips through.

So, that was our few days in Door County. Can you picture it the way I described it? I hope so. I hope, too, that part of my happiness finds its way into your heart...there's more than enough for both of us.

(((((((((((((((So many hugs)))))))))))))))) and so much love,
   Marilyn

Marilyn's e-mail to Paula, Ed and the boys . . . after returning from our trip to Door County—

Good morning, my darlings,

(sigh) So we're back to e-mail, I guess. Not that that's a bad thing, you understand, it just doesn't compare to waking up and seeing you all there, getting those hugs and kisses in person, actually seeing the faces that I love so much.

Thank you for yesterday. It was a lovely day for me in many ways. I have to tell you that last night's church service was something special for me, even more than the morning service—and I can't explain why, really, except that it left me feeling peaceful, and I still feel it this morning. Maybe, for now, that's good enough, right?

Ed, hearing you sing again made yesterday special, too. I know how much it meant to you. I don't know or care WHY your voice got better, I'm just happy for you, and for me. I love the sound of your voice, singing, speaking, whatever. I hear your emotions in it, your joy, your passion, your humor, your tenderness; it all comes out in your voice. Maybe that's why I have to listen to your sermons over and over before the message sinks in, at first, I'm just lost in the sound of your voice and the message doesn't register.

Kiss and hug each other for me. I'm on my way to the dog park and then the gym. Can't wait to get back to both places.

So much love to all of you.

Marilyn

Two days later, Marilyn received an e-mail from her friend, Nancy, from Pennsylvania, whose imagination was running wild with potential explanations for why Marilyn hadn't written lately. Among her possibilities were one, Marilyn had become engaged to a wealthy, romantic man. Two, she was expecting a change-of-life baby; and three, she had been asked to run for governor of the state of Wisconsin. The humor accomplished its intended purpose— Marilyn immediately wrote back the next day . . .

Marilyn's e-mail to her friend, Nancy—

How did you know!!!!!!!!!!! You were absolutely right in your guesses about what's been happening here!!!!

Yes, there IS a new man in my life, although I'm not engaged to him. And he is romantic.

Yes, a baby is involved, although the words "change-of-life baby" have a whole different meaning than the one you intended.

And, as a matter of fact, they DID ask me to run for governor of the state of Wisconsin again, but I turned them down, again. *wink*...

Marilyn broke the news to Nan. She loved telling the "story," as we referred to it. So many times in the first six months that we knew each other, the "story" was still fresh news to everyone, and telling it caused chins to drop, hot tears to flow, and people to cry, "Oh my goodness, what an unbelievable story!" Nothing got Marilyn more excited than the opportunity to retell it again and again.

Reading Marilyn's e-mail reply to Nan reminded me of how carefully Marilyn had studied me the first night we met . . .

Marilyn's e-mail to her friend, Nancy—

...The greatest, most miraculous connection turns out to be that he's "me!" There's nothing of his father in him, he doesn't look like his father (he looks like Joe), he doesn't sound like his father, and he certainly doesn't act like his father. Even in his mannerisms, there's nothing of his father, and believe me, I watched for it!!

...I've gained not only a son who I've come to love as much as I love my other sons and a daughter-in-law/daughter/friend in Paula and two grandchildren, but I've lost something, too.

I've lost the deep, dark secret, I've lost the fear of that dark place in my mind, because they're gone, really gone. I can actually think about that time in my life, if I want to, although I still don't remember much about it and don't see any reason to dig around for those memories. You have no idea how that makes me feel.

A few days later, Paula and Marilyn exchanged the following e-mails:

Paula's e-mail to Marilyn—

It is after 9pm and I just put the kids down and I just wanted to say how much I thoroughly enjoy you in our lives! I am so glad that you are a part of our every day lives, and not just on the fringes. You are soooo... special to all of us.

I love being around you, I love being with you, I love talking with you, I love staring at the fire with you, I love drinking coffee with you, I love watching the sunrise with you, I even love watching baseball with you, get the picture!!<grin>

I guess I just love YOU!!!

Love, Paula

Marilyn's e-mail to Paula—

This one's just for Paula!

Good morning, my precious girl,

I woke up this morning and found last night's e-mail from you; it brought tears to my eyes. Paula, I love all those same things about you, but there's more. I love that it's you who's the mother of my grandchildren. They're wonderful boys and I know they didn't just "drop out of the womb" that way, to borrow a phrase. <wink>

I love that it's you who's the wife of my son. More than anything, I want happiness for him, and he has it with you.

I love your intelligence. I'm proud for you for all the successes you've had, but I'm not surprised. I know you can do anything you want to do.

I love your humor. And I love that you "get" my humor, that laughter is part of what we have together.

I love your sensitivity and thoughtfulness, how you seem to anticipate every need and wish that I have, how you, and you alone, understand completely what all of "this" has meant to me.

I love the ease I feel with you, that our silences are as comfortable as our conversations.

I love your beauty. Sometimes, when I walk into your church, for instance, and see you walking toward me, I'm amazed again that such a lovely, elegant creature is part of my life.

And I love that YOU love ME, that our friendship isn't based ONLY on what brought us together, that we're Paula and Marilyn, two individuals who were put here to add something to each other's lives.

Get the picture? <<<<< smile >>>>>
(((((((((((Hugs just for you)))))))))))
So much love . . . Marilyn

I had been looking forward to the upcoming holiday—Mother's Day. I wondered what it was going to be like for Marilyn. Obviously, it would be different than any other year now that she knew me.

Even still, I was speechless when I received her letter . . .

Marilyn's letter to Ed on Mother's Day 2000—

To my dear son,

I've tried a dozen times in the last few days to write this letter to you, to mark this most special Mother's Day, but for once, the words wouldn't come. Everything I put down seemed to be tinged with sorrow, doubt, regret and that isn't what I wanted this letter to say, because I'm not feeling any of those emotions today. Instead, it's only pride, joy and love that make my heart swell when I think of you. So let me try one more time to tell you, on this day, what it is that I feel.

I feel pride in the man that you've become, with no help from me. You did it all by yourself, you and God. You've made yourself into one of the finest human beings I've ever met—honest, good, gentle, fair, dedicated and committed to what you believe in. The thought that someone like you has ANY connection at all to me makes me proud, and that you should be my son, MY son, is almost more than I can comprehend. I watch you, I listen to you, and everything I see and hear fills me with wonder and awe.

I feel joy when I think of you, joy that you ARE my son, joy that this extraordinary thing has happened to us, joy in all that you brought with you; my darling Paula, your incredible children. I nearly laugh out loud with joy when I think of you, your humor, your intelligence, your tenderness, your wonderful mind, heart and soul. Your very existence delights me beyond words.

And mostly I feel love for you today, and always. It's a mother's love for her son, a love that no longer surprises me, a love that grows deeper and stronger every day, a love without reservation, a love that

I trust, and a love that has its permanent place in my heart.

I feel your love for me too, in every smile, every hug, and every word, in everything you do. I trust that love, too, even though it took some time for me to be able to believe it could exist, to believe that it was always there, to understand that it isn't diluted by resentment and bitterness.

So, on this, our first Mother's Day together, even if it IS a made-up, commercial holiday, I want to tell you two things, that I love you, Ed, my beautiful, amazing son, and that any prayer I pray today will be a prayer of thankfulness and gratitude.

With all the love that's in me,

Your mother, Marilyn

It was an incredibly touching letter to receive. I was also thankful—thankful that, despite my many shortcomings, Marilyn was seeing something wonderful in me. That something—I knew—was not just me, but the Holy Ghost living *in* me.

Marilyn wasn't only thinking of me, however, on Mother's Day.

For a long time afterwards, Paula carried a copy of the following letter in her purse, pulling it out to read whenever she needed a lift in her spirit . . .

Marilyn's letter to Paula on Mother's Day 2000—

Dearest Paula,

Sometimes, to mark a special occasion, I write letters to my children. Today I've already written one more letter than I usually do, and now, I'm writing a fourth one.

What a unique place you have in my life!!!! And to think that a few months ago, you weren't a part of it, I didn't know that "you" existed. Except that, in a way, you always did exist for me, because...

If ever someone had asked me to describe the daughter I never had, I would have described someone beautiful, thoughtful, loving, kind, someone I could have that one-of-a-kind mother/daughter relationship with, someone with a sense of family, someone I could be proud of, someone I would love so very much. I would have described...you.

If ever someone had asked me to describe the daughter-in-law I wanted, I would have described someone who would love and support my beloved son, who would be his soul mate for life, who would be the catalyst that would bring two families together, someone I would love so very much. I would have described...you.

If ever someone had asked me to describe the person I would want to be the mother of my grandchildren, I would have described someone sensible, thoughtful, firm when she has to be, soft when she can be, someone who will give her children a foundation for life, who will enjoy them, and who is willing to share them with me, who trusts me with them, who knows that I want what she wants for them, someone I would love so very much. I would have described...you.

If ever someone had asked me to describe what I wanted in a friend, I would have described someone who is intelligent, fun, loyal, sensitive, compassionate, someone willing to share what's in her heart, and willing to listen to what's in mine, someone who feels the same indescribable "click" of friendship that I feel, someone I would love so very much. I would have described . . . you.

So, there you were!!!...all along, hiding in a corner of my heart, just waiting to come to life for me, and now here you are!!! The depth and strength and unexpectedness of my love for you still surprises me. I love you in so many ways, my dearest girl, and this Mother's Day seems like the right time to tell you that...again.

With all my love, Marilyn

Our relationship was now developing a nice routine. Paula and Marilyn would spend time with each other during the day, getting together for morning coffee, or going out to lunch—all the things lady-friends do with one another. I told Paula if she continued to go out to eat with Marilyn at the present rate, I would have to start hawking *Slurpies* on the third shift at *7-Eleven* to cover the cost!

We were also seeing Marilyn three times a week at church. There were some nights during the week, however, that were impossible to schedule time together because Paula and I were teaching Bible studies. Not since our talk in Wausau did I ever mention again that I thought Marilyn would benefit from a home Bible study. She knew it was available to her so I didn't want to push the issue; I simply waited until she was ready to ask.

"Honey, wasn't that a good time last night?" I'd say offhandedly to Paula within earshot of Marilyn. I wasn't trying to manipulate her, but I wanted her to know that studying the Bible was fun.

"Yeah, it sure was."

Marilyn would become curious and say, "What? What did you do last night?"

"Oh, we had a couple over that we're teaching a Bible study to and we just had such a great time. It was really fun! And, *man*, is God ever doing some neat things in their lives!"

"Oh, really?" She'd respond.

I knew it was just a matter of time . . .

Marilyn's e-mail to Paula—

Hello, my dears,

I hope you're all bright-eyed and rested this morning, but I suspect Monday morning came a little too soon, or rather, Sunday night ended a little too late.

Thanks, though, for answering my questions again last night. I always come away from conversations with you with something else to think about and spend the night getting up to scribble more notes.

(big sigh) I guess what I'm learning is what YOU believe, but I don't think I'm much closer to figuring out what I believe, what I WANT to believe, what I CAN believe. Understand what I mean?

In some ways, my "non-faith" is as strong and unshakeable as your faith, and if that's the devil at work, as the preacher said last night, well, I've got a list of questions about that, too.

I do have faith in one thing, though. I have absolute confidence and faith in YOUR faith. In all my life, I've never seen faith in action as I see it in both of you. It's a wonderful thing to behold.

So I hope you understand that when I ask questions, elementary, awkward, naive, even skeptical questions, they're not meant to try to topple your faith, but to ask you to show me the foundations of your faith. That's the one thing I'll NEVER question, the faith that you have. I know it's real and that I'm still only scratching the surface of it. Every time I talk to you, I find out that it's deeper than I ever thought.

I love you all so much, and mixed in with that love is admiration, respect, and a little awe at what I see in you...

"Wow!" I said to Paula, after reading Marilyn's letter, "I think she's starting to see it."

"It sure seems like it!" Paula agreed, "The next step is a Bible study!"

We love to teach Bible studies to people, I thought to myself. *When we were attending church growing up, we had had little or no understanding about what we believed or why. Now we realize the importance of studying the Bible, and more importantly, obeying it.*

Unfortunately though, many people, just like we were, are content to blindly repeat the traditions of their family's religious heritage, claiming a church affiliation without the slightest idea why. And in so doing, they miss out on a multitude of God's blessings, costing them the most fulfilling relationship they could ever have. They trade relationship for religion, unaware of the responsibility that every person has to seek out God's will for his life.

It's not in my job description as a Christian to ramrod the Bible down a person's throat. Nevertheless, I could not deny the unquenchable passion I had to share God's Word with Marilyn, for I had seen first-hand the results of what happens when a person earnestly runs hard after God.

It's with that approach that we nurtured our bond with Marilyn— not beating her over the head with scripture, but allowing the Holy Ghost within us to display the love of God. We continued to pray that she would develop a hunger for what we had.

"So tell me about this Bible study you teach," Marilyn said, one day.

"Well, it starts with Genesis and goes through Revelation," I said. "You know how so many times people will pick up the Bible, flip it open and start reading but they haven't a clue what it all means? They can't pronounce the names and places and it seems like such a mystery? Well, this study teaches you the Bible from a historical, cultural, and doctrinal perspective as you follow it through chronologically from beginning to end," I went on, summoning all my years of sales experience to help me close the deal. "By the time we're finished, a person has a good understanding of how it all fits together, like the pieces of a puzzle. They realize that the Bible's not that complicated after all."

She nodded her head, musing.

"So, how are you doing with the studies you're teaching right now?"

"Great! Actually we're on the second to last lesson with one and about ready to finish up the other," I said, trying not to give away my excitement. *I knew it! I knew it! She can't keep coming to church and listening to preaching tapes without it getting a hold of her! Here it comes!*

"Well, when you're done, I would like it if you would teach me—that is, if you have a spare night during the week."

Yes! Yes!

"Oh sure, that would be fine," I said matter-of-factly, slowly exhaling the breath I'd been holding. "How about we start next Monday night?"

Marilyn's e-mail to Paula and Ed—

Hello, my darlings,

Couldn't sleep last night, thinking about things we talked about.

By the way, one of the other questions that I brought up that you couldn't answer, and said you would maybe look into, was the question about the Tree of Life, why was it there in the Garden of Eden at all, if Adam and Eve were supposed to live forever?

I spent most of the night trying to figure out what it is that I'm having such a hard time with as we go through this Bible study, trying to put it into words. So let me ramble a bit here, let me see if I can tell you, or, even if I can explain it to myself.

First of all, I know I said I would try to suspend my disbelief, or, at least, that's what I HOPE I said, that I would TRY to suspend my disbelief. That's what I'm trying to do, as hard as that is for me. I'm willing to agree that there really WAS a Garden of Eden, for instance, that God really DID form a man out of clay, breathe life into him, that this IS a book authored by God, that all the other unbelievable things that the Bible says happened, really did happen, and I'm willing to agree to that because the Bible SAYS they happened. That's faith, isn't it? Or the beginnings of faith?

I think I understand how faith is supposed to work. You say faith should come first, putting aside doubt, or most of it anyway, and the rest will follow, the understanding, the clarity, the sureness, the joy. But that "putting aside doubt" is so hard, and maybe a little dangerous. I feel as though I'm trying to twist and bend my mind into a shape it doesn't want to go into, a shape it's never been in before. I am afraid to bend it too far, afraid to relax for a moment because it could snap back into the way it was before.

It feels as though I need to have some foundation, some brace, something to lessen the tension, to help this bending and twisting form a permanent shape, one that isn't going to snap back the first time it's bumped. What better support than the Word of God Himself, right? It still goes against everything that's within me to use the Word of God to PROVE the Word of God, but that's what I'm willing to try to do when I say I'm trying to suspend my disbeliefs. Thus, this Bible study.

I'm not sure what it was I expected to find when I cracked open the Bible for the first time. I was already making a big leap by saying that there IS a God, that He did author this book. I was prepared to try to believe every word. I guess I thought this Bible study would be a matter of you explaining the unfamiliar language and grammar, of you showing me the support for all that you believe, that it would answer any question, that it would be black and white with no gray areas. I thought the Bible would be perfect, that every word would be there for a reason, and that all the words one needed to read would be there. How could it be anything less than perfect, after all, it's God's Word, right?

And maybe that's the way it is. I just can't see it yet. I don't have such a problem with the things that AREN'T in the Bible—at least, not so far. You used the example of Jesus' childhood, how there is almost nothing to tell us about that. It would be interesting to know about that, but it seems as though God didn't think it was important enough to write about, that it wouldn't add anything to our understanding of Him. And I can be satisfied with your explanation of how the generations after Adam and Eve came into being, even though it seems to be a matter of interpretation more than fact, and

I'm not entirely comfortable with THAT idea. Even that Tree of Life question is only interesting, and the answer, or not having an answer isn't going to change much about how I feel about this, as a whole.

I don't mean to beat a dead horse (Wonder if THAT particular cliché came from the Bible?)...If the Bible is perfect, if it's really God's Word, those words must have been used for a reason. If we are to do, or not do, precisely what the Bible tells us, even if it's stated only once, why not that? I still don't understand. I nod my head and tell you that I see what you mean, and I do at the time you're telling me, but every time I come home, think about it and come up with the same questions: Why is that piece of Scripture there at all? What are we supposed to believe about it? Why can we treat it differently than other pieces of Scripture? If we're allowed to question, are we allowed to choose any answer that feels right to us? Isn't that interpretation? And, the Big Question, is the Bible perfect or isn't it?

I know it's a small point and I don't want to make more of it than it deserves, or be stubborn about it, but I suspect there will be more points like this one. And these points are all tiny drops of doubt, inconsistency, confusion, that I didn't expect to find. I don't want those tiny drops to wash away this foundation I'm trying to build. And I CERTAINLY don't mean to try to undermine the foundation you have; instead, I'm trying to figure out what your foundation is made of so that I can build one just as strong.

Maybe this question, and other questions like it, will gnaw at me always. I guess I'm just hoping that there will be enough answers to other questions, enough vision that will come of all this, that a few inconsistencies won't matter. But right now, this scares and worries me a little. Maybe some day I'll look back at this note and wonder at what I was thinking, why didn't I see the truth. But right now, I'm just holding on, trying to bend and not let go.

(sigh) I don't know if ANY of this makes sense. Maybe I'm just rambling and it won't seem so important after I take a nap. And I don't think I've told you anything I haven't told you before—I just needed to say it again.

Love to all of you,
Marilyn

I had to be on my toes every Monday night. Everything was fair game. Everything was open for discussion—every scripture, doctrine, topic, or command was subject to Marilyn's torrent of relentless questioning—just as it should be. Each question seemed to generate two more. Many times I would make a statement that begged to be qualified, and it would send us hurling through the Bible in search of scriptural support. It was as if she was saying, *Don't just tell me it's a brick—show me the whole wall that it's part of!* She was an awesome Bible study student!

We proceeded slowly and methodically. It was the perfect playground for her intellect, a place where she could exercise her mental reasoning. Marilyn was quick to describe herself as one who *refuses to check her brain at the door.* That can only go so far with the Word of God because the Bible is a book that not only requires belief, but also faith. Hebrews says, *But without faith it is impossible to please him: for he that cometh to God must believe that he is...*

Like a fledgling about to leave the comfort of the nest, Marilyn would soon have to spread her wings and lunge out into an unknown realm—the realm of faith.

Marilyn's Letter to Ed . . . on his 35th birthday—

Dear Ed,

I don't have a birthday card for you today. I looked in a dozen different stores at a hundred different cards, but every card written for a child, a son, spoke of the joys and rewards of raising a child. So I swallowed hard and put them all back in the racks.

I'm having a hard time writing this letter today, too. I can't get it to say what I want it to say, and I can't stop it from saying what I don't want it to say.

I didn't expect to have such a difficult time with your birthday. I thought I was finished with the "regret" thing, but I guess I'm not. You said this morning that 35 years have zipped by. For me, your 35 years are crammed into six months, such a small chunk of your life.

I can't help wondering about the other 34 birthdays and the years in between them. I'm learning about you, learning what has made you YOU, how you got to be who you are, but it's only bits and pieces, really, and sometimes those bits and pieces don't seem to fit with the person I know. I realize there's no changing the past, but it doesn't stop the wondering from sneaking in.

Now, that's what I DIDN'T want to say today, but there it is. That's what came off my fingertips today.

Here's another stab at what I REALLY wanted to say:

It seems impossible to me today to think that the day of your birth, June 8, 1965, should be almost completely erased from my memory. It's the day that changed my life, more than any other day ever has. It's the day I received a wonderful gift from God, and I'm recognizing more and more that that's exactly what it was, what you are.

Sometimes, when I watch you, listen to you, hold your hand, think about you, the questions come; I wonder who you are, why you were put here right in front of me, right now, why did all the pieces come together right now, what's really going on here?

And the only explanation I can see is that you are what you are— a wonderful gift from God, a gift that I received on June 8, 1965, but didn't see, didn't start to unwrap, until six months ago when the blinders were taken away from my heart.

As for the other questions, I don't think I know the answers yet, but I'm eager to try to figure them out.

I was told by a very wise person recently that a true gift doesn't have to be earned or reciprocated, but the better the gift, the more you want to do exactly that. So, here's what I'm going to do, to try to be worthy of my beautiful gift:

I'll love you for the rest of my life, tell you so, and show you that I do.

I'll encourage and support everything you do simply because I know that the kind of person you are makes everything you do the right thing to do.

I'll try to bring something into your life that maybe only I can.

I'll try to live up to whatever image you had of me all your life.

I'll try to make up for any pain that I caused you.

I'll try not to dwell on the regrets I have from time to time and instead enjoy the miracle just as it is.

And, most of all, I'll try to remember every day to thank God for the gift of you, God, who is becoming more and more real, but who becomes the most real when I look at you.

June 8th, your birthday, remembering the day of your birth, the *blank places in my memory being filled with feelings of joy, gladness, thankfulness and love.*

June 8th, 2000, your 35th birthday, our first together.

Happy birthday, my beautiful, amazing son, my most precious gift.

With all my love today and every day,

Your mother, Marilyn

Again, Marilyn touched my heart with words in a way no other could. What she didn't realize before writing this birthday letter to me was that she was *already* doing many of the things she said she would strive to do!

Marilyn's e-mail to Ed—

I got home from church a while ago, experiencing my usual Sunday night "buzz." I love Sundays in your church. I don't completely understand the things I see happening, but I know that I'm witnessing something out of the ordinary, something I want and need to know more about.

Ed, I loved your sermon "I Ain't Wearing No Polyester Leisure Suit" tonight. I loved the delivery. So did everyone else. I loved the message, although I'll have to listen to it again because I still get too caught up in watching the messenger to completely get it the first time. I even loved that it was delayed a week so that it was even more appropriate tonight than it would have been last week. I loved listening to people talk about it later.

I love seeing you so involved in your church. It's your natural element and I can't imagine you any other way. I know you consider what you do to be a huge responsibility, but you wear that responsibility well.

Dearest, that we met at all was a huge surprise to me. That we formed this wonderful relationship which is so necessary to me now has been a bigger surprise. Even more of a surprise has been discovering that this son of mine is so immersed in a church, any church, and that it almost completely defines who he is.

But, most surprising to me, a fact that I never would have believed even if I could have been convinced that all of the above would happen some day, is how much I love that about you. You might never be able to really appreciate what that statement means because my "disbeliefs" are probably as foreign to you as your beliefs were to me.

I don't mean that my acceptance and love for all of this are any credit to me, rather, I think it's part of this great big miracle that's happening. It's the part that caused my eyes and ears and heart to be opened so that I COULD accept and love what I'm seeing.

I don't know what's at the end of this path I'm on. Just a few months ago, I didn't even SEE the path, and certainly didn't know there was a destination I needed to head for. But now I'm beginning to see something off in the distance and I think I want to take a look. The path is a little unfamiliar, though, and I'm really glad I have your hand to hold along the way.

All my love, Marilyn

With all that had happened, it was hard to believe it was now only six months since we met for the first time. Marilyn was circumspect and needed to share it with someone outside her immediate family circle. She e-mailed her friend, Lori—a twenty-five page chronicle of "the story!"

Marilyn's e-mail to her friend, Lori—

Hi Lori,
   ...this has been the MOST incredible year of my entire life, and that's not an exaggeration...

   And I don't just mean it's been incredible because cumulatively a lot of things have happened to me, I mean that the individual things that have happened have been some of the most important events of my life. And you're part of it, not just as someone I spew it all out to, but in a more active way.

   Talking to you, listening to you talk to me, reading and absorbing your poetry, laughing with you, encouraging you and feeling encouraged by you, feeling free and (semi-)intelligent when we talk about the most unlikely subjects, feeling respect, love, concern going both ways between us. Even when we don't talk every day, or even every few days, I always know you're there, and I thank God for that.

I mean I REALLY thank God for that. I did that last night. Ed and Paula and I went to church again at the family camp I told you about. I stood there between these two people that I love so much thinking again about how this all happened, and I almost can't believe it.

I listened to the same preacher we heard on Sunday night. Never mind his awesome delivery; it was simply uncanny hearing the words he said. He talked about things that have been going through my head lately, even used the some of the same words I use when I think about it all. He talked about things that Ed and Paula and I have talked about in just the last week or so—"Spooky," as Ed would say, because the subjects weren't the usual run-of-the-mill subjects; they were pretty off-the-wall, but there he was!!...talking to the three of us.

Well, I guess you would have had to have been there to really appreciate what I'm telling you. I know it sounds like I've gone 'round the bend, Lori, but it all fits the pattern of my life lately, and that's never happened to me before. Everything fits, even the "bad" stuff seems to have a purpose and a reason for being.

So, anyway, it seemed like I should be saying thank you for all of this, and God seemed to be in the neighborhood, so that's Who I thanked.

Love you, Lori.
Marilyn

One of the characteristics that immediately endeared Marilyn to me was her intellect and hunger to dig out answers to questions. One night, as we watched *The Sound of Music*, she wondered aloud how Austria could have a Navy, being that it's landlocked. The next day she sent me this e-mail:

Marilyn's e-mail to Ed—

I was so curious and puzzled about Austria having a navy that I did a little digging.

Turns out that until the end of WWI, Austria was part of the Austro-Hungarian Empire, a monarchy. The empire took in a big chunk of Eastern Europe mostly to the east and to the south of what is Austria today. The part to the south had a long coastline on the eastern side of the Adriatic; thus, the Navy.

The empire was dismembered after WWI and, since Austria no longer had a coastline and no need for a Navy, Captain Von Trapp lost his job...

Thought you'd like to know the answers. I know I'll sleep better tonight having solved these mysteries. <wink>

Her "need-to-know" was actually an unexpected blessing to me. I was preparing a sermon and remarked in passing that I was trying to recall a quote that went something like: "I have met the enemy and it is I." It should not have surprised me when an e-mail from Marilyn came the next day:

...Here's the answer...

In the 1800's, Commodore Perry announced a victory by saying, "We have met the enemy and they are ours."

In 1971, Walt Kelly who wrote the Pogo comic strip used a paraphrase on an Earth Day poster. He said, "We have met the enemy and he is us."

Love you...Marilyn

I'm not aware of any preacher who has a personal research assistant, but I now had mine! Even better, the line of demarcation between Marilyn's journey with me and the one she was about to embark on with Jesus, was slowly being crossed . . .

Marilyn's e-mail to her friend, Nancy—

Hello, Nancy,

Sometimes it almost scares me.

When I say it almost scares me about how important to me they are, what I mean is that I'm not sure how much of what I'm doing-- reading and studying the Bible, going to their church, trying to feel God's presence, walk with Him—is because of God, and how much is because of them, trying to understand them, be close to them, be like them. Is it God I feel I need, or is it THEM? Do you know what I mean?

I don't know how to sort that out, what questions to ask myself about that. I haven't tried to fool anyone, them or myself, about why I began this journey, it WAS to try to understand them and be close to them. But, now, it's turning into something else, I THINK. And that's the crux of my question, is this "something else" real, or am I fooling myself, trying to convince myself?

That's my biggest struggle these days, and maybe is what's holding me back from REALLY feeling God's presence.

But just so you know, I'm not letting these questions diminish what's happening. I'm pretty sure the answers will come, or maybe I'll find out in the end that the answers don't matter, that, if I get to wherever it is I'm going on their coattails, it won't matter HOW I got there...

It was the moment we knew would inevitably come. She finally stood face-to-face with the question: *Is this incredibly wonderful change in my life totally because of Ed, or is it because of something greater?* For weeks she wrestled with it. The question demanded an answer.

God's timing is perfect. How could Marilyn possibly know that the next day after e-mailing Nancy, God would supply it? The battle, the fight, the clash between the exercising of her faith and the stronghold of her disbelief was about to come to an end. *Let God arise . . . great victory awaits!*

Marilyn had lived without Him in her life for over fifty years, her joy overshadowed by the darkness from her past. But I had served God long enough to know that He never changes—*it's in our darkest times that His Light shines the brightest.*

Chapter 8

July 23, 2000
Fox Cities United Pentecostal Church
Menasha, Wisconsin

*T*he preaching was incredible. Reverend Harold Linder from New York City was ministering in our Sunday morning and Sunday night services—and the messages were hitting people straight in the heart. Not only that, there was electricity in the air as the presence of God surged through the sanctuary while the congregation sang out during the worship service. So it was appropriate that that morning Rev. Linder preached on *The Privilege of God's Presence*, encouraging people that their hope and joy is found in the presence of God.

He finished his message by inviting people to come down to the front altar area of the church to pray. Marilyn had never done this before, but this morning she had a look of determination on her face as she stepped out of her pew and made her way down the center aisle.

We knew without a doubt that if Marilyn could *feel* the real and tangible presence of God, then she would find the answer to why we were different. She would discover the key unlocking the mystery of what her soul had longed for all these years. She would realize that no matter how wonderful the relationship she was forming with us, in no way could it compare to a touch from the Master.

The experience she had in the morning service of physically feeling the presence of the invisible God proved to be only a prelude to an even greater blessing that she would receive at the evening service.

That night, after preaching another powerful message, Rev. Linder came down from behind the pulpit during the altar call and stood directly in front of us. A beautiful melody from the musicians filled the air. People all over the building were reaching out to God, seeking answers for their lives. Paula and I moved in next to Marilyn. As others crowded in around us, we began to pray that God would touch her in a special way.

With her eyes closed and her hands raised in worship, Rev. Linder gently and lovingly placed his hand upon Marilyn's forehead and began to pray a blessing over her. Hot tears finally poured from her eyes. As he prayed, the presence of the Lord intensified within our small circle of praying people until I felt as if my knees would buckle!

I looked at Marilyn and could see her mouth moving in prayer and her chin begin to quiver uncontrollably. Her lips stammered as the move of God heightened around us, people shouting out praises of joy to God in loud voices. The crescendo of worship was thunderous, reverberating throughout the sanctuary.

Then God performed the greatest miracle in the history of all mankind: He filled her with the Holy Ghost! Marilyn began to speak in an unknown tongue as the Spirit of God caused the utterance—just like people received in the book of Acts!

The look of joy on her face was unmistakable. I'd seen it hundreds of times before, and I had experienced it *myself* hundreds of times before. Marilyn had gone beyond *feeling* God's Spirit—she was now *filled* with it!

Marilyn's e-mail to her friend, Nancy—

...So, anyway, there I was, in church on Sunday morning, with a copy of your e-mail tucked away in my purse, to be read over and over. There was a guest preacher that morning, a man from New York who is spending the week at their youth camp to preach to the teenagers every night. The last thing that Ed said to me before he started preaching was that I would enjoy him because he's heard him before and he knows I enjoy the wonderful speakers I'm hearing.

Well..."enjoy" was an understatement, if I ever heard one. The scripture he used was Psalms 16:11 "in thy presence is fullness of joy." That's something I've been struggling with, seeing and feeling His presence in OTHER people, in church and elsewhere, but not really able to feel it for myself, as if a clear wall separates me from that experience.

The wall cracked a little while he was speaking. I knew God was speaking to me, for me, through his words, and for the first time when everyone went to the altar to pray at the end of the service, I went, too.

But it didn't end there. The preacher immediately came down from the platform, and in a crowd of 200+ came directly to me, put his hand on my head, and prayed for me. He prayed for ME!!!!!!! His words weren't generic, could-have-fit-half-the-people-in-church kind of words, they were specific to ME!!!!! And I DID feel the presence of God, I knew He was real, and I knew He was there...

So I went home and cried for the rest of the afternoon. It was too much to talk about, even to Ed and Paula. I have to say I don't remember WHAT this man said, his actual words, but I remember how I felt. And, in my mind, that's some kind of proof to me, me who needs proof before I can believe anything, that this wasn't just a charismatic speaker who pushed the right buttons in me, and that this was real only in my mind...

So, that was Round 1. Round 2 happened at the Sunday evening service. Same speaker, different scripture, same incredible experience. He used many scriptures, but the subject was, why we go to church, what are the reasons we go to church. Sound like a question you've heard before????? In fact, copies of our Saturday e-mails were still in my purse.

Again, it was all for ME. Again, I was drawn to the altar. Again, he came down to me and prayed a prayer that he couldn't possibly have known was tailor-made for me. And, again, I felt God's presence, even closer than before!

...We're going up to the camp tonight to hear him again. And, while I don't expect to re-experience what happened on Sunday, I learned a long time ago not to walk into church casually. Something ALWAYS happens in church, sometimes in only a very small way, and sometimes in a big way, like Sunday.

I told Paula last night that I love going to church, can't wait until the next time. I told her that there's CHURCH, and then there's *everything-between-church. And now, I'm even learning to take church home with me, to carry it with me...*

If I could point to the one thing that allowed Marilyn to break through to receive the baptism of the Holy Ghost, it would be when she made the statement early in our Bible study that she would "suspend her disbelief." When she finally stopped trying to figure out everything about God and stopped requiring an answer to every unknown in the Bible, she then began to walk more by faith, trusting God with what He promised He would give her. By suspending her disbeliefs, she allowed God to prove He is real and that He is faithful to follow through with His promise of pouring out His Spirit upon all flesh. She was a real-life example of Hebrews 11:6 that says, *...He is a rewarder of them that diligently seek Him.*

And reward He did! For the next week, Marilyn was a different person. The most notable change was her countenance. Before, she looked serious, reserved, and oftentimes sad—but now the smile on her face never left. She was lively when she talked, punctuating her words by moving her hands in animation. There was a bounce in her step as if she were on her way to do something exciting. It was obvious to anyone who knew her that something was indeed different!

Nancy was nearly as excited as Marilyn about her spiritual awakening, celebrating and rejoicing right along with her. God was now another aspect of their relationship that they had in common and Nancy wanted to know every detail of what happened to Marilyn . . .

Marilyn's e-mail to her friend, Nancy—

Dear Nancy,
I love hearing from you. I love running to the Bible to look up the scriptures you share with me. I love your joy in my joy. I love that I can talk to you about these amazing events that are happening in my life right now.
But please don't feel that you have to reply to everything I write. Sometimes it all just bubbles up and boils over, becomes more than

my mind can handle and I have to put it in writing to sort of see it for myself—to see what actually comes off of my fingertips when I open the connection between my heart and my fingers. And so, I'm using you. I love being able to share all of this with you because I know you understand it and rejoice in it, but it's for me, too...

So much love, Marilyn

Marilyn's e-mail to her friend, Daniel—

...I DO kiss J and D [Joe and David] more than I ever had in the past...tell them more often that I love them...because I DO love them so much...and now I'm not taking that for granted.

Loving this new son makes me love J and D even more because I know what I missed with Ed...and I didn't miss it with J and D. I have memories, treasures and thoughts stored up about them that I don't have with Ed and I'm more aware than ever now how important that is.

Not only was it an exciting time for Marilyn, but for me as well. God had been dealing with me for a long time concerning a call on my life to the ministry. I had such a tremendous respect for a God-given call to preach that I moved at a snail's pace, not wanting to fully admit it was possible. I was scared to acknowledge it for fear that I would embarrass myself if God wasn't truly calling me.

It started way back during my stint as our Youth Director and intensified the year before Marilyn and I met. As is the case whenever I need help sorting through the spiritual stuff, I sought my pastor.

"I'm feeling the need to deliver the mail," I said to Pastor Yonts one night after service, a reference to preaching the Word. Pastor Yonts is known for giving layman in the church the opportunity to step out in ministry. Because of that, he continues to add to a growing legacy of God-called, young preachers that have trained under him and are now doing great works in the kingdom of God.

"Alright. How much notice will you need to be ready to preach?"

"Well, I guess two weeks would be good."

"No problem, Bro . . . I'll let you know when."

Less than one month later he would contract a deadly lung disease, be placed on life-support, and be put into a drug-induced coma for three weeks, his life hanging by a thread.

While Pastor Yonts was in intensive care for the next three months fighting for breath, the responsibilities of the church fell on our Assistant Pastor at the time, Danny Sharp. To help lessen the burden on him to preach three times a week, another man in the church and I took some of the services.

I had preached before, but this was different. I was surprised at the new-found passion that came out of me. I felt like a different person! It seems God knew exactly the precise moment to place within me that burning desire to preach—just when it was most needed.

One of the reasons my faith was so strong about what God could do in Marilyn's life was because of what I witnessed Him do for my pastor. After a long, arduous battle, he miraculously recovered, even though his family had been told on two separate occasions that he had only hours to live. He's now a living, breathing example of a divine healing of biblical proportions. The book written about his miracle, *"With Every Breath I Praise Him!"* is a must-read! When he finally returned home and was strong enough to have company, I went to talk with him.

"You know Pastor, I think I'm now to the point that I think it's a possibility that God is calling me into the ministry." I said, stammering and struggling with fear of acknowledging what others had said was obvious to them. *What if I'm wrong?* I thought.

He just gazed at me, shook his head and said, "You're called."

"But do you mean . . ." I began to debate, "Yeah, okay," I exhaled a long breath.

"Whew, it sure feels better to get that figured out!"

When I came home and told Paula, she looked at me with a "Welcome, you finally made it!" look on her face.

"I've known God was calling you. People in the church have known." She said, "It was only a matter of time before *you* finally acknowledged it!"

Yes, finally, I knew—*God was calling me to be a preacher!*

By the time I met Marilyn, I had already been training under my pastor and fulfilling all the requirements of our organization to become a licensed minister. She was intrigued by it. She constantly bombarded me with questions about how I got my sermon thoughts, or how I got this or that out of a particular scripture. I could rest assured that on Monday Bible study night I was due for a long discussion on the fine points of anything I preached previously on Sunday.

At times, I thought Marilyn knew my sermons better than I did! Occasionally she would even chastise me for saying something that contradicted what I had preached over the pulpit. She became my biggest supporter. The Bible was a limitless source of treasured conversations for us. Entering the ministry was one of the most memorable times in my life, and Marilyn was right there to share it with me.

Marilyn's e-mail to Ed and Paula—

Dear Ed and Paula,
Did Solomon write Ecclesiastes? Or did someone else write it? Is it ABOUT Solomon?
One source I found says there's disagreement about whether Solomon actually wrote it and whether it's about him. Sure sounds like Solomon, the little I know about him. What a fascinating guy!
Did I tell you how much I love this Bible study????? I do more and more. You were right Ed; the "history" part of it is so interesting. But so is the "human" part. I stumbled over Ecclesiastes last night on my way to somewhere else and I never did get to wherever it was I was headed. I found Ecclesiastes pretty depressing, to tell you the truth— seems wisdom isn't all it's cracked up to be.
I know I'll love the Bible more and more as time goes on. Right now, I love it because it's a good book, as a piece of literature. This past weekend, Ed, I listened again to your sermon, "The Book of wonders," because I wanted to see if I heard anything new in it this time around, especially since we're in the midst of this Bible study— and you're right, it's many books, a science book, a psychology book, etc., etc., etc.

I don't love the Bible yet for the reasons you both love it, or at least, that's not the overriding reason for why I find it so fascinating. The history/science/psychology/etc./etc./etc. gets in the way. I love discovering something familiar, seeing the context, understanding what the words really were intended to mean. I love the stories, the "characters," seeing them as they originally were intended to be seen, not corrupted by someone else using them to make a point. But right now, I have to keep reminding myself that I'm reading the "Word of God," know what I mean? The spiritual part hasn't quite kicked in, maybe.

But in the meantime, maybe the beautiful, interesting, and surprising words and stories and characters are the "hook" that keeps readers' attention until the real love of the Bible starts to burn. (big sigh) Or maybe I'm just reading the Bible to avoid vacuuming and dusting this morning. <wink> (Sorry, Ecclesiastes' what's-it-all-for influence showing again.)

But anyway, I want to thank you both again for taking the time for this Bible study, and for doing it so well. Ed, I really do appreciate your way of explaining, of speaking in pictures, of making it seem "real," of making it fun.

And Paula, you know what I'm going to say to you, don't you? I love the way you always seem to know what I'm really asking, where I'm headed, and even WHY I'm asking. But that seems to be true of everything you and I have together. You always know how it is. Solomon could have taken a lesson.

The next time we saw each other, I answered the question: "Yes, Marilyn, Solomon is credited with writing Ecclesiastes" (and he sure would be proud of you for seeking so hard after his wisdom!)

Soon after, she would enter an emotional and spiritual battle. Marilyn hadn't been herself lately Agitated, Irritated. She acted like everything seemed frustrating and repulsive to her. She was just plain struggling.

You don't have to serve God long to recognize that once you decide to commit yourself wholly to God—in any area of your life—spiritual resistance is sure to follow. And when that resistance comes against you, it's hard to understand. Only later can you look back and realize the reason for your struggles—hindsight being a wonderful thing. The devil is content to let us go along and "play church" as long as we don't sell out in obedience to the Word of God. He doesn't mind us "window shopping" for truth—as long as we don't buy into it—but be assured, as soon as we decide to surrender our lives to Jesus Christ, every devil in hell suddenly snaps to attention at the sound of warning bells and prepares to launch an assault on our minds! It's the spiritual equivalent of the timeless transgression in playground football of "piling-on," and Marilyn was not immune to it.

Paula and I were concerned about Marilyn, but we also knew that times like these were not uncommon—actually they are to be expected—and are part of the Christian maturation process. Discovering how to fight her battles through prayer was a lesson she would need to learn to help carry her through the rest of her life . . .

Paula's e-mail to Marilyn—

Just a quick note—you know we are here for you when you are ready to talk! We LOVE you and CARE about you!

We don't want to interfere but are very concerned. I wanted Ed or me to call you to tell you these things, but he feels we would be pestering you...and we don't want to do that—therefore, this e-mail from me <grin>

You know, when you don't know anything about what is bothering a person you love and care about, the mind has a heyday! Anyway, we love you!

Love, hugs and kisses!
Paula

Ed's e-mail to Marilyn—

Fourth and goal, ball on the three, down by five, one second left on the clock...

Overtime, one second left on the clock, down by one, two shots from the free throw line...

Bottom of the ninth, behind by three, bases loaded, two outs, two strikes, about to get the 3-2 pitch...

...don't quit.
Love, Ed

When she called me after receiving my note, she sounded better. We had been praying a hedge of protection around Marilyn for the last few weeks and it was starting to work.

But prayer wasn't the only thing that helped—we would sing a little chorus at church that goes like this:

When I get in His presence, when I get in His presence
Every doubt that I face in a moment goes away
When I get in His presence, when I get in His presence
When I get in the presence of the Lord

I knew without a doubt that Marilyn wouldn't stay in the valley she was now walking through. *Why?* The answer was simple. Because Marilyn continued to be faithful to every church service, and even though she didn't *feel* like worshipping God, she did it anyway. *God's greatness and worthiness is not predicated on how we feel, good or bad—He's simply worthy of our praise and worship!*

When I saw that Marilyn disciplined herself to be thankful in *all* things and worship the Lord for who He is and not what He does, He began to fight her battle for her. She did her part and fought through the spiritual heaviness every worship service by lifting up heavy hands that hung down and singing with a voice that desired to be still.

At some point, she must have learned to bring into captivity every negative thought, subjecting it to the God's presence, because Jesus swept over her soul and peace flooded her heart. It was then that she was able to claim victory!

We had a particularly good Bible study the next Monday. For months now we had been plowing slow, deep furrows through the Word of God—and it was obvious that Marilyn was considering the necessity of applying the Word of God to her life, not just simply studying it. It occurred to her that she wasn't merely learning facts and stories, but gaining a real understanding of what God was requiring of her. The Holy Ghost was revealing much, and therefore much was now required. It was not simply enough to hear and read God's Word—along with revelation came responsibility.

Marilyn was about to take the next step in her relationship with God . . .

Marilyn's e-mail to her friend, Nancy—

Good morning, Nancy,

I've made up my mind. I'm going to be baptized. You're only the second person I've said that to. I wanted to tell you first, but it slipped out when I was talking to someone yesterday. I guess Ed and Paula are assuming, hoping, praying for that, but I haven't yet said the words out loud to them.

I don't make decisions quickly. I think about things for a long time before I make up my mind. But, when I do, I don't look back, don't second-guess myself. So, I know it's safe to tell you this. I know it will happen.

If anyone had tried to tell me even a few months ago that I would be joining a church, any church, I would have laughed out loud. I might even have been offended. And, if I somehow could have been convinced that I might join a church, and that person had told me that it would be THIS kind of church, I can't imagine what I would have said. I know I would have used the word "never" in my response.

But I have to tell you, Nancy, that everything I hear and learn and experience makes sense to me. It fits. I'm learning to separate what's really me from what's connected to Ed and Paula...and I know that my agreement to suspend my disbelief was the right thing to do, because now that doubt has simply evaporated.

...First, I had to figure out what I believe, be convinced that my beliefs are real. Why would I obey Someone I don't believe in, obey the Words of Someone I don't believe in?

So, that's why this is such a big deal for me. It represents more than just joining a church. I know I'm not the first person to figure that out, but for me it's light years from my thinking just a short time ago.

...I'll write soon, my friend. I owe you a long letter. I've started it many times, but when I go back to it, I always find my thoughts have

changed. Until now. I think I've turned a corner here and come face to face with the truth.
So much love, Marilyn

October 22, 2000
Fox Cities United Pentecostal Church
Menasha, Wisconsin

Physically, I was feeling terrible—I'd been battling the flu for days and couldn't shake my fever of 102°. Nothing, however, was going to keep me from being at church. When Marilyn told us of her decision to be baptized in Jesus' Name, we were ecstatic— especially because I would have the honor of baptizing her!

By the time I arrived, I knew my fever had started to break because I was drenched in a cold sweat. I seemed to be gaining some strength but my body felt like it had been used as a punching bag. I toughed it out through the service, and finally, it was time for Marilyn to change into the long, waterproof robe used for baptizing people. She stepped up on the platform to where the baptismal tank was located, and I helped her slip into the water. Pastor Yonts handed me the microphone and I began to address the congregation.

"For those of you who don't know, Marilyn is my birth mother," I explained.

"I was adopted when I was six weeks old. We met back in December this past year and God has done a great work in our lives. I want to make note of the irony, I guess you would call it. She was obviously involved with my birth thirty-five years ago," I said as we smiled at each other. "And today I get the opportunity to take part in her *new* birth thirty-five years later."

The congregation erupted with shouts of praise, clapping and cheering. I gave a few quick instructions to Marilyn and we were ready to go.

"Marilyn, upon the confession of your faith, and your repentance, and your desire to be obedient to the Word of God, I now baptize you in the Name that is above every name, in the Name of Jesus Christ for the remission of your sins. In Jesus' Name!" I called out.

When Marilyn came up out of the water she began to vocally worship and praise the Lord, her hands raised toward heaven. Those of us gathered around the tank joined her by also praying and rejoicing. A beautiful look of joy and peace was upon her face. The presence of God was touching her, just like it had on the day she received the baptism of the Holy Ghost.

After she got out of the tank, Marilyn went into the dressing room to dry off and change. While we waited for her to come out, the man recording the event pointed the video camera at me. I smiled and gave him a "thumbs-up." A few minutes later, Marilyn exited the dressing room to applause, the congregation still excited about her baptism.

"So, what do you think?" Paula asked her.

She raised her hand, like me, giving a "thumbs-up"—and replied, "In a nutshell!"

Marilyn's letter to Ed—

Dear Ed,

Do you remember your first words to me? Of course, you do. They were "thank you." They were your first words to me after your birth. And, while these may not be my first words to you after my re-birth, that's what this letter is about.

Thank you for baptizing me—a short little sentence that sums it all up.

You baptized me, the "you" that is my son, the "me" that is your mother. Sometimes I've wondered if I love you too much. Maybe you do, too. But I think I HAD to love you as much as I do, you HAD to come to me as the person I see, brilliant, beautiful, wonderful, shining in my eyes, so that there could be no ignoring you, so that I couldn't possibly overlook you or any part of who you are. Can't you just imagine God finally getting fed up, finally saying, "Okay, you silly woman, ignore THIS!" and then touching us with this miracle that still brings tears to my eyes?

What happened to me on Sunday was something I never want to forget, never want to take for granted. I know that repentance and baptism in Jesus' name were only two parts of this miracle, but they were important parts for me. As I told you, they involved a choice, a decision on my part, a commitment, an admission that I not only COULD live my life for God—but that I SHOULD live my life for God and, most importantly, I guess . . . that I WANT to live my life for God!

Thank you, my darling son, for more than just taking part in the act of my baptism.

Thank you for teaching me what I need to know in a way that I can understand, with a mind that is becoming as familiar as my own—patiently, gently, intelligently, with your love for God so apparent that any doubts about His existence simply vanish.

Thank you not only for explaining to me what God's Word says, but for showing me how to use it, how to live a life according to it. Thank you for showing me in a way that is the only way I could understand and believe it, by seeing it in you every time I look at you, hear your voice, or think of you.

Thank you for being that perfect ambassador, for doing what you do out of love for God and for the people you meet. I keep thinking that God MUST be pleased with you, that you must be what He had in mind right from the beginning.

So I was wondering, how DO you thank someone who works so hard to save your soul? What's the etiquette here? Do you shake his hand? Do you send flowers? Do you bake him a pound cake?

Nothing seems like enough. No words seem like enough.

I guess I'll just give you and God the one thing that I know you both want from me, a promise to try to live my life according to His Word. I can't do anything more and I can't do anything less.

With so much love,

Your mother, Marilyn

Many of Marilyn's letters that she had written me previously touched me deeply, but none was more satisfying than this one. *Praise God!*

Marilyn's e-mail to her friend, Nancy—

Dearest Nancy,

...What to tell you about next????

My baptism, maybe? "Awesome" is a very much over-used word these days, but it describes the experience. I only wish that I had been more "present" for it, more aware of every part of it. I saw *pictures taken as it was happening and people have talked about it, but it's almost as though none of it registered.*

I was thinking this morning about what I wore that day and I can't remember! But maybe that was my way of making it what I always thought it should be, something just between me and God...

...I spent the few days beforehand crying and I really couldn't tell you why that was. Maybe it was the fact of leaving something behind and not being sure what that was. Maybe it was the repentance part of it. But I know that this was the first deliberate decision I had made in a long time. Lately life has just been sweeping me along, but this was different.

And when it was over, I couldn't remember what it was I had been sorry to leave behind. Everything DID seem fresh and new. I really DID feel like a new creature. It's a feeling that's lasted and will continue, I think. It certainly has changed my perspective on just about everything...

Marilyn signed off her e-mail to Nancy with this: *Marilyn, the newest sheep in the flock.*

A month later, it would be Thanksgiving, and what a special day it would be! Although we had been consistently grateful as the year progressed for what God had been doing in our lives, Thanksgiving was a day we could slow down long enough to be truly circumspect—stopping to catch our breath and take inventory of all that had happened over the last year.

We were coming up on the one-year anniversary of our meeting, and so much had changed for all of us that it was difficult to remember our lives before knowing each other. The blessings came so fast and furious it was like trying to take a drink from a fire hydrant. We didn't mind, however,—we counted those blessings one-by-one as they arrived and stacked them neatly in a special storeroom in our hearts.

Each one us—Marilyn, Paula, and I, had many reasons to be thankful. Some of those reasons we shared in common—others were personal to us, individually. Of all the blessings to be numerated, the one that ranked the highest with Paula and me was that Marilyn had embraced Jesus Christ. True, our relationship was something rare and special, but in light of what God did for her, it paled in comparison.

I think Marilyn even saw me in a different light. She had finally come to understand that my proper place was not upon a pedestal, but alongside her, at the feet of Jesus . . .

Marilyn's letter to Paula . . . on Thanksgiving Day 2000—

Dearest Paula,

When I last saw you, when you stopped and had lunch here on Tuesday, one of the things we talked about was Thanksgiving.

Thanksgiving Day has always been a special day for me. It's not only a day for family, friends and good food, but I use it as a marker, a day to look back at the past year and compare this Thanksgiving to last Thanksgiving, and to all the Thanksgivings in the past.

I really do give thanks on Thanksgiving Day, I always have. Don't ask me Who I was thanking, though. I wouldn't have been able to tell you. But this year, Thanksgiving Day will be like no other. I DO know Who I'm thanking. And that, in itself, is the first reason to give thanks, isn't it?

Marilyn's e-mail to Paula, Ed and the boys . . . on November 30, 2000, the one year anniversary of the phone call that led to our meeting—

Thursday, November 30, 7:00 AM . . .

One year ago...I didn't even know your names.

So much love, Marilyn

Chapter 9

February 2001
Menasha, Wisconsin

D ays went by so quickly—then weeks and finally, months. So much had changed for all of us in the last twelve months that it didn't seem possible for it to continue at the same pace. It had been a magical whirlwind of a year—a honeymoon time, a Camelot. As wonderful as it all was, we desired for life to slow down a little to give our emotional rollercoaster a much-deserved break. The coming year would prove it was not to be the case.

Marilyn's e-mail to Paula and Ed—

Thank you for my whole life... for giving me peace with the past, joy in the present, and hope for the future and beyond.
I thank God for you today and every day. I thank God for the miracle of who you are. I thank God that you're my son. I love you, Ed.
Life is good. Love, Marilyn

Life *was* good. Marilyn decided it was also a good time for her to begin downsizing her life. For nearly thirty years she had lived in the house she and Danny had purchased. A wealth of family memories had been created there so she felt it was appropriate to sell the house to Joe, ensuring its passing into another generation of family history.

Paula happened by a nice duplex one day while out running errands and asked Marilyn if she wanted to check into it. It was perfect: a modest-size kitchen and living room with two bedrooms, perfect for entertaining a few friends and family members. And the best part: it was only about a mile from our house! Within a few weeks Marilyn had signed the lease and moved in. We were now practically neighbors!

Marilyn's e-mail to her friend, Nancy—

...Big news first...I've moved. Phone number is the same...

It's a duplex. The landlord lives on the other side and he does all the stuff I don't want to do. He's tripping over himself to make sure I'm happy here. I think I love him. LOL

It was gratifying to see Marilyn's relationship with God blossom and grow. One area of her life where this relationship manifested itself was her compassion toward others. By nature, she had always been one to give or to do for others, but now she did it as unto the Lord. If somebody had a need; babysitting for their kids, a meal to be cooked, or an ear to bend, Marilyn was there. Her servant's heart was as big as any in the church. She took ownership in the kingdom of God which included not only the church building, but the church members. And even greater than that, she was now feeling confident and compelled to share her walk with God with other people outside of her network of church family and friends . . .

Marilyn's e-mail to her friend, Lori—

Hello, Lori,

...Lori, I should know this, but I don't remember—senior moment, I guess. What is your mom's first name? I don't want to do anything you aren't comfortable with, but praying is the only thing I can do for her. I'd like to submit a prayer request for her and have our church pray for her, too. Is that okay?...

(((((((((((((((((ANOTHER ENORMOUS HUG FOR YOU)))))))))))))))

I miss you now...more than ever.

Love, Marilyn

Without fail, if there was a church-related project to be done, Marilyn was the first one to show up . . .

Marilyn's e-mail to her friend, Nancy—

...I'm more and more involved in the church and I love that. I spent part of today at our pastor's house...washing windows. They're on vacation and we're finishing some remodeling and doing some heavy cleaning while they're gone as the church's gift, along with the Pastor Appreciation Banquet next week.

The week before Mother's Day, Paula and Marilyn went to a ladies' retreat which provided yet another precious moment.

It was held in Appleton in the same hotel where Danny's sport's banquet had been held for years. The first night of the retreat, there was a Minister's Wives' dinner that Paula planned on attending while Marilyn had dinner with some lady friends from our church. After receiving directions to where the dinner was being held, Marilyn walked down to the lobby with Paula. They were about to part ways for the evening when Marilyn stopped to stare at Paula, a little grin forming on her face.

"What?" Paula said, puzzled.

"Do you realize that we're standing in the exact spot where you first saw me?"

"Oh, my goodness! It is!" Paula exclaimed as they both hugged and started laughing.

"I love you, Marilyn."

"I love you, too."

It was the same spot where Paula and her mom purchased their tickets from Marilyn for the sports' banquet more than six years before.

The summer continued, filled with retreats, church camps, and revivals. Yet, every so often, the demons of her past—fear and depression—would rear their ugly heads in defiance of all the miracles that were happening in Marilyn's life. The need to face-off with her demons once and for all was nearer than either of us knew, but for now Marilyn employed the weapons of warfare that helped her most—prayer and worship. What she learned through her struggles, she freely passed on to help bless others . . .

Marilyn's e-mail to her friend, Tim [Nancy's Husband]—

...As for me, I've had my ups and downs. I went through a few weeks' stretch of something. Depression, maybe, although Ed called it "oppression" and I have to tell you that that sounds like a good word for it. It would come and go, hit me like a physical force, making it seem hard to stand up straight and take a deep breath...

...I have to tell you about an amazing experience I had as a result of whatever-that-was. I had been talking to Ed and Paula about it and they were worried about me, of course. Finally, one day in church, when even my hands felt too heavy to lift in worship, Ed, who is an elder of the church, did as James 5:14 directs, anointed me with oil and prayed over me for the oppression to lift, and it did!!!! I could feel it lifting as he prayed. I could feel it in my shoulders. I could stand taller, I felt lighter, and I could breathe. I'm not saying it never came back, but it never came back as strongly and never lasted as long. And remembering that experience seems to ward it off when I feel the beginnings of it coming back.

This experience has helped me, not just to lift the oppression, but to give me a better understanding and appreciation for prayer and healing. That's been a stumbling block for me, something I haven't been able to grasp, for some reason. But what happened to me was so real that I can't deny it or explain it away.

Last week Paula and I and the boys went to Family Camp in the woods in northern Wisconsin. Ed came up for a day or two. It was, to use an over-used word, awesome! Prayer in the early morning, Bible teaching all morning with the most incredible preacher, lazy afternoons of fellowship (and napping), and then church at night with another anointed preacher.

The presence of God was so strong that it gives me goose bumps to think of it, even now. It was as though there was a bubble over the whole place and the world couldn't intrude.

I love what's happening to me, love this journey I'm on, and I love having you to share it with—both of you...

With my deepest love and appreciation that you're in my life. I hope we can catch up on the details soon. In person would be nice, don't you think? ((((((((((((((Hugest hugs))))))))))))))))...
All my love, Marilyn

What I didn't realize was that I was about to go through my own dark times. Pain and suffering was close at hand.

A good friend of mine who pastors a church in a small town about an hour away asked me to come preach for him on a Wednesday night. It's a wonderful group of people that I've grown fond of, having preached there on numerous occasions. We had a great night worshipping God and fellowshipping together, but by the time service was over, and we had gone out to eat afterward, it was late. Paula and the kids fell asleep on the way home and I was relaxed and content—I felt the service had gone well.

I was surprised when I drove up to the corner that we live on and noticed my brother's car parked in our driveway. *It's eleven o'clock at night during the work week! What is Mike doing here so late?*

When we got out of the car I could see by the look on Mike's face that it was something serious.

"Hey, what's up?" I asked, trying not to sound nervous.

"We need to talk."

"Alright, come on in."

We went into the house, turned on the lights, and hung up our coats.

"Can you put the kids down before we talk?"

"Sure," I said, realizing it must be something sensitive if it needed that kind of privacy. My initial thought was that he wanted to talk about a personal problem of some sort.

When the boys were tucked in and prayed for, I went downstairs and sat on the couch across the room from Mike, who was sitting in a big, oversized chair.

"Well, what's going on?"

Mike has always been hard to read, and I could see he was struggling with how to begin. I waited patiently until finally he spoke.

"Jesus decided to take Jimmy today."

"What? . . ." I said. A shudder of panic shot through me. "What are you trying to say?" I demanded, not trusting I heard him correctly.

Surprisingly, I never considered my father, who had been on dialysis for years now, as well as the transplant list for a kidney. Five months before he had undergone quadruple bypass heart surgery. It seemed to be one medical problem after another—as if he was falling apart piece by piece.

Mike repeated, "Jesus decided to take Jimmy today."

In a flurry, my mind began a process of convoluted reasoning. *No, it can't be true, not Jim! Mike's wrong! Somehow he's mistaken. Jim's young, energetic! He's not unhealthy or overweight—and he's only thirty-two years old!* A sick nausea passed through me in waves. Psychological defense mechanisms kicked into emergency high gear, shielding me from the harsh reality of Mike's words, while the lump forming in my throat threatened to choke off my breathing.

Don't beat around the bush, Mike! Just say it! Just say he's dead! I was irritated, even though the situation wasn't his fault. I wanted him to slap me in the face with words I had no chance of rationalizing. There had been no warning—I couldn't believe this! I needed to hear the raw truth, and at the same time, pleaded within myself to not hear it at all.

"I came home from work tonight at seven o'clock and the police were at our apartment," he explained. "They asked me if Jim was my brother. When I said, 'Yes,' they told me that Andy (Mike and Jim's roommate) had come home and found Jim still in bed."

It was true. My little brother was dead. He had gone to bed and never awaken—arrhythmia had stopped his heart.

The inevitable had finally happened. For thirty-six years I had avoided the gut-wrenching pain that the death of a close, immediate family member brings—until now.

I thought back to a phone call I received a little over a year before Jim's death. One Saturday morning, my friend Doug, called to tell me his father had succumbed to cancer.

His parents didn't have a pastor and the family asked if I would do the funeral. I only had my ministerial license for a month. I recall telling Doug that I would be honored to officiate his father's funeral, and that I would do my very best; but I had to confess, that although I sympathized with him, I just didn't know what he was going through because it had never happened to me. Now my experience had caught up to my responsibilities.

Marilyn's help during this trying time was invaluable. The duties of the arrangements for the funeral fell largely upon Mike, Paula and myself. My parents were devastated and could only be expected to offer a limited amount of help.

Predictably, Marilyn immediately went into high gear, preparing meals, running errands, watching Jordan and Jonathan when necessary, and consoling my parents in a way that neither I nor Mike were able to. Through it all, Marilyn was there, blessing my family and helping to ease the terrific hurt that death brings.

I was now changed, having felt the "sting" of death. After Jim's death, I would never look at life, in all it's fragility, the same way again.

Not long after the funeral, Marilyn and I were invited by a local adoption agency to speak to prospective parents about our relationship. In the course of answering their many questions, inevitably, we had to address the issue of my birth father. Talking about "him" to total strangers proved to be the start of something I never expected.

"You know, the last two years have been a honeymoon," Marilyn said to Paula one morning while they were relaxing, having coffee in our living room. "I feel it's time to face up to some of the bad stuff."

Paula sensed she knew what Marilyn was referring to.

"I wanted to know if Ed's birth father was still alive, so I looked up his name in the phone book and it was there. I called the number and the answering machine picked up. It had his voice on it—I'm *sure* it was him. So I drove past his house, and Paula, it just didn't fit. It was a beautiful house with beautiful landscaping. If I would have pictured where he would be living, it would be above a bar or in a dumpy, old trailer," Marilyn said incredulously.

"I want to go to the courthouse to do some digging to find out if he's changed, and I'd like you to go with me to help. Would you do it or would you feel like you were betraying Ed by helping me?"

"Yes, I'd love to help, and at this point I don't feel like it would be betraying Ed, but if it gets to that point, I will tell you," Paula said.

Marilyn's e-mail to her friend, Nancy—

Hello Nancy,

...I went to a workshop for a reason, [a birth mothers' convention in Milwaukee] to try to resolve something I'm struggling with. That's the question—"mystery" maybe is a better word—of Ed's father. Ed and I did a presentation at an adoption agency a few weeks ago, and because I knew people would have questions for me, I thought about things that I haven't thought about lately.

One of them was Ed's father. And then I asked Ed what his feelings were about that—was he still so angry, or was he curious, what? He said he IS curious, not like he was about me, but because it would complete the story, in a way. As it is, there's a piece missing.

And I have to admit to some curiosity, too. I'd just like to know what happened to him. But even more than that, I wonder how accurate my sketchy memories are. Where did some of Ed's unfamiliar, but wonderful, characteristics come from?

But I'd like to know anonymously. I couldn't take the chance of him ever knowing about me. I'm still too scared. The thing is, I'm the only one who knows his name and, if I died, the secret would die with me and Ed would never know. Some part of me feels like I owe him that information. And I love him enough to want to give him the one thing that no one else can give him.

On the other hand—and there's always an "other hand,"—I'm just selfish enough to not want to rock the boat. I love the way things are between us and I don't want anything to change. Once I say the name out loud to someone, it's out of my control and that scares me.

Anyway, that's why I went to that workshop, to see if anyone had had any experience with a situation like this. No one did on a personal level, but the facilitator did have some advice, she said to look into it, and how to go about it. I'm not sure if I'll take that advice, but that's another of the bits of clutter in my mind these days...

While Marilyn wrestled with the issue of my birth father, breaking news was coming in from all sides of the family. David announced that his girlfriend, Suzette, was pregnant—due around February 2002, and Joe announced that he and Katie were engaged to be married in September 2002.

Marilyn and Paula began their search for my biological father at the courthouse in Green Bay. Again, much like my search for Marilyn eighteen years before, public records provided pieces of the puzzle. In this case, though, it turned out to be a roaring avalanche of information—and just as devastating. It eventually got to the point that they had no choice but to confront me with what they were doing.

Considering how terrified Marilyn had been of "him" for all these years and her steadfast desire to never go near him again—she vowed the first night we met to never tell me his name—I was a bit surprised by the news. On the other hand, with the strength that God had placed in her life to deal with her toughest personal issues, I saw this mission as her way of slaying the arrogant Goliath that had taunted her most of her life; therefore, I was okay with what she was doing.

A week after Marilyn and Paula went to the courthouse, the three of us got together again so they could update me on what they had found.

"We found a lot of information," Paula announced. I could see from Marilyn's body language that this was hard for her, so she got Paula to deliver the findings of their search to me.

"We were able to trace the family tree; he's divorced and has one daughter. He spent time in prison and his criminal record is long, but it seems to stop as he gets older," Paula said.

She detailed what they learned of his family history and then chronicled the trouble he'd been in throughout the years. I silently listened, riveted, appalled—my brow deeply furrowed. When Paula was finished, Marilyn finally spoke.

"I was confused by the fact that he lived in a nice house and that his criminal activity dropped off. I thought maybe he had changed," she said. "So I looked up his ex-wife's phone number and had Paula call her." Marilyn had the sound of regret in her voice.

Paula had been on the phone for about an hour with the woman named Adeline. Adeline had been more than willing to tell it all. Unfortunately, what Paula heard was more dreadful than any of us ever wanted or expected.

"Then she told me I should call her daughter, Mary Jo—your half-sister," Paula said, "that she would be able to tell me even more."

Paula had also called Mary Jo and spoke to her for an hour. If I had been disturbed before by what I was hearing, it was only a prelude to what we would learn from Paula's conversation with Mary Jo. According to Mary Jo, nice house or not, he apparently hadn't changed much.

"Are you okay, honey?" Paula asked after she finished talking.

"I don't know," I said in a whisper. Marilyn wept silently on the couch.

I was shocked beyond words by what Paula had related. Wave upon wave of warm nausea passed through me, making my stomach turn, agitating like a washing machine filled with churning, putrid water. *Oh, God, help me! This is too much to bear!* Rage boiled up inside me—a human pressure cooker threatening to blow—because I was helpless and at a complete loss to control the things I was hearing. When I saw what all of this was doing to Marilyn, it infuriated me further.

He's a monster!—a one-man wrecking ball that cuts swathes of destruction through people's lives! Worse yet, he's my biological father!

"Your sister was very nice. She talked freely about all this stuff, even though I wouldn't give her our names," Paula said. "She's been estranged from him for years. She's also excited about the possibility of meeting you. I got the impression that family is very important to her."

I wanted desperately to ignore this half-sister—after all, she was the flesh and blood of "him." I was prepared to take out my frustrations on her because of who she was. *So what if she offered up information? So what if she wants to meet me?* The bitterness threatened to rise up in my throat like acid—until I realized that I was no different. I, too, came from him. And just as God has preserved me by His mercy and grace to become the man I am today—in spite of my biological heritage—it was entirely possible that she wasn't anything like him either. At the least, I owed her a phone call.

Calling Mary Jo was like experiencing a case of déjà vu. I had never had a sister, and similar to the night I first met Marilyn, it felt like I was an actor in a play. Notwithstanding, I liked her immediately. Perhaps she quickly endeared herself to me because of her openness and transparency.

Mary Jo told me things about the biological father that we shared, and my broken heart went out to her, for only the hardest of hearts could listen to her detail a troubled childhood and not be moved to compassion.

By the time I hung up with her, I knew we would eventually meet. It took only forty-five minutes of talking with Mary Jo to feel a bond begin to form. I wanted to meet my sister less because of curiosity and more because of the love I now felt for her. It was going to feel strange to be this close to "him," but I knew, as I did with Marilyn, that God had divinely ordained our coming together. Something good was about to happen!

Marilyn spent the night on our couch. We all needed to be together. For days afterward I struggled with my feelings. I was disgusted with myself every time I looked in the mirror. I could not get past the thought that every feature, every facial expression, every facet of my personality was in some way, large or small, due in part to "him." I felt polluted and dirty, trapped in a body made up of his DNA.

Even worse were my thoughts—I wrestled with a guilty mind. How could I possibly stand behind a pulpit, a man supposedly called by God to preach the gospel of Jesus Christ, and have these types of thoughts racing through my mind? My heart was torn asunder—one part reluctantly acknowledging that my biological father had a part in my existence, the other part resenting him for how it happened.

Somebody asked me sometime later if I would like to meet him. "It would not be good for his health for us to meet," I responded. The truth was I wouldn't know whether to thank him or punch him!

Mary Jo and I met at a restaurant a few days later near their home. It turned out that Mary Jo and her husband, Brad, lived only thirty miles away from us. When we faced each other for the first time, I immediately noticed Mary Jo's eyes. Normally, Paula is the one to pick up on people's physical features, not me; but there was no mistaking those blue eyes—they could have been my own looking back at me.

Only one of their two boys was with them, the other being at school. I was now the proud uncle of two handsome little nephews—Justin, eight, and Brandon, four.

We spent a long time together and had a great time getting to know each other. We had started our conversation over breakfast, and after a few hours the waitress was asking if we were going to order lunch! Our first meeting had been an absolute success.

A week later, when Paula went to Mary Jo's house for lunch, she mentioned that I would be preaching the next Sunday. With some hesitation Mary Jo said, "Do you think he would mind if we came to hear him preach?"

Marilyn's e-mail to her friend, Nancy—

...if God wasn't part of my life and I didn't have Him to help me, this [finding out about "him"] would have nearly killed me. I've shed gallons of tears and sent up volumes of prayers. Sometimes I feel as though I'm 20 years old again and all alone, except that I'm not alone this time. Ed, in particular, has been extremely sensitive to my feelings and it's brought us even closer together. My biggest fear was that this would somehow damage our relationship, but that hasn't happened.

The part about feeling a burden for this girl [Mary Jo] is true. It was about as close to a clear answer from God as I've ever gotten. I was praying about it in church one evening when she was only a name on a birth certificate, and Ed still didn't know about her...wondering and asking if I was doing the right thing for Ed by even considering the possibility of bringing her into his life...and the very next thought in my mind was not about Ed but about her...that it was for HER that I was doing this.

And, sure enough...after they met only once...she wants to come to church to hear her brother preach. I have to almost chuckle because that's what drew me to church for the first time...

Mary Jo, Brad and Adeline came to church a few weeks after we met. I was scheduled to preach the evening service. Like with Marilyn's first time, it wasn't my intention to preach hard just because they were there—it just happened to come out that way.

Again, like it happened with Marilyn, I came down off the platform soaking wet from sweat. I had spent all I had in me in thirty-five minutes. As I approached the pew where they were sitting, I noticed Adeline had tears streaking down her face. I faced her, kneeling on the pew in front of her. Before I could warn her about my wet shirt, she seized me in a huge bear hug.

"I'm kinda wet..." I began to say, but it didn't stop Adeline. More déjà vu—it hadn't stopped Marilyn either.

We pulled apart, and she took my hands in hers. Looking shell-shocked from the power of the presence of God that she must have been feeling, Adeline gazed at me through watery eyes and said enthusiastically, "I could get into this! I could get into this!"

"You *need* to get into this!" I replied. "*This* isn't just having church; *this* is God tugging on your heartstrings to get your attention. *This* is the Spirit of God you're feeling."

"Ohhh, my...I guess it is," she said.

I moved over to Mary Jo and Brad. I felt led to pray over Brad because he suffered from chronic back pain due to a previous workplace injury so severe that it required seven major surgeries,

"Brad, I have seen many miracles over the years, so I believe in the power of prayer," I said. "I know you're really hurting and I was wondering if you would mind if I prayed over you, in Jesus' Name, asking Him to give you relief."

"Sure, that would be alright," he said, giving a little shrug.

I laid my hand upon his head and began to call upon the Name of Jesus, praying that God would bring instantaneous and divine healing to Brad's body. The presence of God was so strong around us! The expression on the three of their faces told me that they had felt it, too. When I was finished, we all looked at each other lovingly.

"Now let's just trust God to do His work," I said as we all hugged each other. It had been a wonderful time together.

The Lord made this night happen—more of my new-found family had met my Best Friend—Jesus Christ. No longer was I shocked by what God could do to bring people into a place where they could meet Him face-to-face. My faith soared for those I didn't think could ever be reached. *Look what the Lord has done!*

Two weeks ago I didn't even know my sister existed—today we worshipped the Lord together! This was starting to look all too familiar. I believed it was the making of another miracle.

While we were enjoying getting to know Mary Jo and her family, for Marilyn, it was a source of pain. Although she rejoiced with us, trudging through the long-buried memories of her darkest time was difficult . . .

Marilyn's e-mail to her friend, Nancy—

...It's the hatred, Nancy, that's so hard to bear. People pray around me in church and all I can think is "I hate him, I hate him, I hate him." It's getting better, but I'm still a long way from where I want to be. I'm learning what real forgiveness and real repentance mean.

...In the meantime, keep me in your prayers as I keep you in mine.

Love, Marilyn

Some wounds can be healed in the blink of an eye. Some deep, slow-healing wounds require the Balm of Gilead to be steadily applied by God's Spirit in prayer, not only for the purpose of restoration, but to prevent them from festering. I was now able to share in, to some extent at least, the pain of Marilyn's past. The question was—would we allow those wounds to stay infected, poisoning the abundant life that God had given us?

"I want to talk to you about something," Marilyn said to me as we were having one of our heart-to-heart talks.

"Sure, go ahead."

"I know you've been hurt by the things you've learned about your biological father," she said, "but I want you to know that I've been praying about him and all that's happened in the past..."

"*And* . . . I coaxed.

"I've forgiven him. It's still hard to think about the things that happened to me, but the result was "you," and that makes it all worth it," she said. "I'd rather he never finds out about you, but if he does, I'm not terrified of him any more."

She waited for my response which was slow to come. Perhaps, thinking I was skeptical, she made certain there was no confusion about how she felt.

"Ed, he's a soul. You're a soul winner, and one day you may be his only hope."

Then she told me his name.

Hearing it, I shuddered as if I had been touched by a hot brand but at the same time, my heart was full. I had prayed a long time for Marilyn to be able to forgive him and now she had finally arrived at that place in her life, thirty-six years later. She was at peace with her past. The deeply-entrenched, long-time residents of her heart—horror, shame, and hurt—were now gone. Only God could have replaced them with love and forgiveness. With the bitterness gone, the capacity of Marilyn's heart could now expand to make room for compassion—compassion for others that Jesus said to bless when they curse you, do good to them when they hate you, and pray for them when they despitefully use you and persecute you. With God's help, *she* had slain the giant in her life.

Marilyn's victory now became my conviction. Although I had prayed for Marilyn to be able to forgive, I now had to do it myself. Admonished by her demonstration of forgiveness, I faced my own giant. If she, being the one to have suffered so greatly for so long, could forgive, how much more should I? But as soon as I attempted to lay it down at the foot of the cross, the devil arrogantly reminded me of the horrible side of my genetic history.

Then the answer came to me—similar to my struggle after Paula made that first phone call to Marilyn many years ago when she denied me. *Spirit of adoption...Spirit of adoption...For ye have not* received the spirit of bondage again to fear; but ye have received the Spirit of adoption, whereby we cry, Abba, Father.*

I realized that, biological or not, he was *not* my "father." My earthly father was the honorable man who blessed me when he adopted me, took me under his roof, and raised me—and my heavenly Father blessed me when He adopted me by the infilling of His Spirit. *...The Spirit itself beareth witness with our spirit, that we are the children of God...* Learning the truth about "him" didn't change a thing! It didn't matter at all—I was still a child of God, baptized into His Name, an heir to all His glory!

Much like when Marilyn had straightened me out on my tendency to apologize for the worship at church, the student had again taught the teacher by exemplifying a heart of forgiveness. It was then that I, too, was able to let go of the anger and finally forgive—a lesson that will benefit me for a lifetime.

Thanks, Marilyn. Again.

Chapter 10

January 2002
Menasha, Wisconsin

*A*s our second year together drew to a close, finishing another chapter in our fairy tale-type relationship, we could again reflect back in amazement at how much had changed. My and Paula's bond with Mary Jo, Brad and their boys was growing. We were now getting together every Friday night for dinner and a Bible study, alternating weeks at each other's house.

Adeline, not wanting to intrude on our budding relationship, was involved in her own Bible study near her house with the pastor and his wife of a Pentecostal church that I had connected her with.

Jordan and Jonathan were growing up to be "little men." Jordan had tried out with the *Appleton Boychoir* the year before, a prestigious group of adolescent boys with angelic voices that perform locally and travel abroad to sing. Jordan, along with fifteen others, was chosen out of hundreds of boys from all around the area. His beautiful voice and innate ability to hear pitch would eventually propel him into the top choir, being promoted as quickly as was possible.

Jonathan was becoming a shining star in the classroom—a real wiz in math and reading. He also continued to hone his social skills with that sweet personality of his. (Every teacher he had from kindergarten on had fallen in love with him!) God had blessed us with two of the most wonderful boys in the world, and Paula and I were finding joy in watching our children grow up to be godly young boys. We were also thankful every day for God's divine hand being upon them.

The advent of the New Year brought with it a new life. In early February, David and Suzette became the proud parents of baby Elijah—Eli for short. Marilyn was now a grandmother of three. It was special to her, having gone from not wanting or needing to be a grandmother, to embracing the role to its fullest. It was one way of lessening the regret she felt for missing out on Jordan and Jonathan's infant years. It was her opportunity to be the doting grandma that she now *wanted* to be . . .

Marilyn's e-mail to her friend, Nancy . . . on Marilyn's 58th Birthday—

Hello Nancy,

I start with an apology for not calling you on the day that I said I would. That turned out to be the day after Elijah was born and I went to Milwaukee to meet him for the first time. I hope you understand.

Since then life has been a little schizophrenic. I've been driving a lot...100 miles south a couple of times a week to see that new little life and 70 miles north a couple of times a week to watch the end of a life.

My brother [Steve] is in the last stages of cancer and every time I see him, I think that it's for the last time...

Two days later, Steve died. James 4:14 says, *Whereas ye know not what shall be on the morrow. For what is your life? It is even a vapor that appeareth for a little time, and then vanisheth away.* So it would seem in this case—Steve was only fifty-four years old.

The celebration over Eli's birth was now tempered by Steve's death. I hurt terribly along with Marilyn—it having been only a little over five months since I lost my brother, Jim. We wept together. We grieved together. We prayed together. And in God we found the strength needed to go on. Paula and I would come to depend on it— for this was not to be the last vapor to vanish away.

"Hello?" I asked sleepily into the phone.

"Hey, this is Mike."

"What's up?" I asked. It was early on a Monday morning about four months after Steve's death, and I hadn't yet gotten out of bed to go work in my downstairs office.

"I'm at Mom and Dad's house. She called—Dad couldn't get up—his legs won't work. I can't get him into the car so I've called an ambulance."

"Alright. Do you need me to come over, or should I meet you at the hospital?" I asked, concerned.

"No, that's okay, I don't think you need to come over. It doesn't look serious. He seems fine except for his legs. I'll just follow the ambulance over and call you from there to let you know what's going on," Mike said. "Mom's got eye surgery in another part of the hospital this morning anyway, so I'll bring her to her appointment first, then call you."

Because of his diabetes, my dad had been in and out of the hospital like a revolving door for the last few years with a myriad of complications. To some extent the family had become desensitized to the potential seriousness of these episodes. It's not that we weren't concerned—it just appeared to be another trip to the hospital, get checked out, and then back home again. I laid there in bed for a few minutes, trying to wake up and gather my thoughts. About the time I was up and almost dressed, the phone rang again.

"Ed, you better get over here fast!" Mike said with a shaky voice. "Dad just went into cardiac arrest!"

"Okay, I'm leaving right now!"

While hastily driving to the hospital, I prayed that my dad would be alright, but hanging over my prayer, was a dark, shadowy thought: *Today is the day I lose my dad.* Shame, because of a lack of faith clung to me like cellophane wrap—and guilt, for thinking like that, mocked me. Yet, somehow I knew.

The moment I arrived, the nurse told us that the doctor needed to meet with us immediately. She led us to a small family waiting room and told us that the doctor would be with us in just a minute. She left, closing the door behind her. The air was still and heavy in the tiny room.

"You ready for this?" I asked Mike.

"I guess."

The door opened and a doctor and nurse entered, inviting us to sit down. It looked so obvious—them asking us to sit down, the nurse there to make sure we would be alright.

"I'm sorry," the doctor said, "but your dad has died."

No amount of foreknowledge could have lessened the paralyzing shock of those words. The man I called "father" was gone—the one who never once made me feel like anything other than his own son was dead. He was only sixty-six years old.

Another wisp of vapor had vanished.

Marilyn's e-mail to her friend, Lori—

Hi, Lori,

...Ed's adoptive father died on Monday morning. Or did I tell you that? My darling boy is having an awful time of it. Worse than when his brother died in August.

Anyway, his mother [Martha] has been staying with Ed and Paula and I've been cooking and spending time with Martha so Ed and Paula can do what they need to do. I changed my plan to go to Milwaukee on Tuesday, and instead I'm leaving this morning for just today. I'll be back tonight...

As she did when Jim died, Marilyn kicked into "servant" gear again. Only this time she provided help and comfort in an area that few are qualified in. Having lost a husband, in particular a husband who had required years of care like my dad had, Marilyn was able to speak to my mom about her own ordeal and the tremendous rush of emotions that accompany the death of a spouse. The pain of death stung us again, so we continued to weep, grieve and pray together, knowing that God was the only One able to bring peace to our troubled hearts.

Two weeks after my dad died, I was scheduled to preach at another church. God laid a message upon my heart to preach for their Sunday night service that would profoundly affect me personally. The story of Job has been preached just about every conceivable way, by the best-of-the-best preachers, but it's never meant as much as it did to me now, considering all the losses I had suffered in so short a time in my family. I didn't preach a message I had heard previously or one I had read—I preached something I lived through.

It was the kind of message I felt I would preach one time and retire it forever. It was entitled: *In All This, Yet Will I Praise Him!* It came from the last three verses in chapter one of the book of Job: *Then Job arose, and rent his mantle, and shaved his head, and fell down upon the ground, and worshiped, and said, Naked came I out of my mother's womb, and naked shall I return thither: the LORD gave, and the LORD hath taken away; blessed be the name of the LORD. In all this Job sinned not, nor charged God foolishly.*

Job had been through the wringer—his life had been squeezed dry. He had lost it all: his cattle, his sheep, his camels, his health, and most troublesome, his ten children. Yet through it all—or in the words of scripture, *In all of this*—Job went through the normal, human grieving process of that day by tearing his clothing and shaving his head in mourning. In other words, having a relationship with God didn't exempt him from exhibiting the pain and suffering a person must bear when tragedy strikes without warning.

That was not the only thing Job did. The scripture says he *fell down upon the ground, and worshiped.* He said, "The Lord gives, the Lord takes away, but *blessed be the Name of the Lord.*"

I had also been scheduled to lead the worship service the day before Jim's funeral and the day after my dad's funeral. At first I was ready to assign it to someone else, but then I decided to go through with it.

On each occasion I noticed that when I got to the pulpit and began ministering in song, the sweetest, most precious and peaceful presence of God touched me. I realized the strength I had been given to press on was greater than I believed possible. Yet, it wasn't my relying on my own human strength—it was my receiving supernatural strength from a loving, gracious God who the Bible says is *touched with the feeling of our infirmities.*

With the death of my brother and my father, I had learned the priceless principle that Job exemplified: It's necessary to mourn and grieve, but true strength can only come from worshipping and praising the Lord in the midst of your tragedy. Though weeping may endure for a night, joy *always* comes in the morning.

It had been over a year since Marilyn had seen Daniel or Nancy—even longer since she had taken a trip. Now, a month after my dad's funeral, she was preparing to do both. Her itinerary included flying to Pennsylvania to meet Nancy and then the two of them driving to South Carolina to meet Daniel. It had been a tough six months, and she was walking on air waiting to go. With everything they had planned it was sure to be a busy time. Even so, Marilyn never intended to take a vacation from God . . .

Marilyn's e-mail to her friend, Daniel—

Good morning, my dear,

Do I need to remind you that I'll be seeing you in eleven (11) E-L-E-V-E-N...that's fewer than a dozen...almost into the single digits...days????????

(I'm smiling with a lump in my throat and my heart beating faster)

Now, about the favor. Can you please make a phone call for me? I hope it's a local one.

I'd like you to call the First United Pentecostal Church [in the town where Daniel lives]. I'd like to know when their services are on Sunday (in particular, Sunday, June 16). Is there an evening service that day, as well as a morning service? If so, I'd like to know what time they start.

Also, I'd like to know if they have a mid-week service and, if so, what day and time (in particular, the week I'll be there)

All three of them had an awesome time and Marilyn returned refreshed and energetic. It had been just the diversion she needed from a breakneck, hectic life of family, friends, and church. It turned into a slow, lazy summer for all of us—which we had prayed for. We had had more than enough excitement in the last two and a half years for the average person, although our story was anything but average. The dull and mundane started to sound very appealing . . .

Marilyn's e-mail to her friends, Nancy and Daniel—

Dear Nan and Daniel,

...I really have nothing to tell you except trivialities. Nothing profound, nothing wise, nothing dramatic. Just me talking to my friends about my day. It was a very nice day.

I went to church this morning and it was good. Ed led worship and sang my most and least favorite song. Turns out, it's the same song: "How Great Thou Art." It's my favorite because it was written for a voice like his and when he belts it out, my knees buckle. I love it. But it's my least favorite for that same reason. When he sings it, I definitely am NOT thinking God thoughts. I'm thinking about the singer instead. Know what I mean?

A friend [Shirley] who attends another church showed up unexpectedly and it was nice to see her. She's another of those people who used to be on the fringes of my life but has become closer lately. Like you, Nan, I always knew she was a Christian but that didn't impress me much until now. And she's also a birth mother who gave up a child many years ago and has since been reunited with her daughter...

Anyway, she and I went out to lunch with Ed, Paula, Jordan and Jonathan, partly to celebrate Jordan's 10th birthday. Today I'm the grandmother of a ten-year-old. He's taken another growth spurt lately and I hardly have to look down at him anymore.

He really is an awesome little boy. Ed and Paula went camping for a few days this week to a place where Ed used to go with his parents. He told me that his best family memories are from that place. This was his first trip back there in many years and, his father having died just a few months ago, it was hard for him. He said Jordan stuck to him like glue (or maybe like a chigger although he didn't use that word) and seemed to understand the significance of this "pilgrimage."

Jonathan continues to make a career out of being cute. He's going to be baptized next Sunday and there will be a double celebration: Jordan's birthday and Jonathan's baptism. It feels a little like this is where I came in. Deja vu, sort of. The first service I ever went to in this church was just the opposite: a celebration of Jordan's baptism and Jonathan's 5th birthday.

...Then it was church again and it was good again...

...See, I told you this wasn't going to be a profound note. Just a description of a typical Sunday. Maybe tomorrow I'll write to you about a typical Monday. LOL Just kidding.

Love, Marilyn

Marilyn's e-mail to her friend, Nancy—

...Speaking of church stuff...I'm feeling a little lonely. The couple that have been my best friends (next to Ed and Paula) moved to Mississippi and I really miss them. She has helped me a lot over the past two years and so has he. I look back at the pew where they always sat and can't believe they're gone.

And next week Amy [a college student friend who spent the summers at Marilyn's house] will be moving out to go back to school. I love having her here. She's even more involved with our church than I am and we talk about it all the time. It's like having church/Bible study/fellowship 24 hours a day when she's here.

So, my bestest friends are gone or going. And maybe Ed and Paula will be next to go. Nothing for sure, but I'm holding my breath at the moment.

A long time ago I asked them to please tell me if anything, however remote, was in the wind so that I'd have as much time as possible to prepare for it...

The thought of his leaving scares me, Nan. I'm not ready yet. I know that this is what he was born to do and that, if it doesn't happen this time, it will some day. So I'll support him completely and not give him any reason to worry about me.

But he's still so new to me. I haven't had enough time with him. He's something special to me in a way that no one else in the world is. He represents my own personal miracle, the one I think about when I need a miracle and begin to doubt that it will happen.

So, I'll be praying real hard about this. I'm not sure what to pray for, to tell you the truth. God's will, I suppose. In a way, that's pretty exciting. God has quite an imagination, so I'm waiting eagerly to see how He makes it all come together...

For weeks, Marilyn had been asking me if we could get together to talk—the kind of quiet, intimate talks she had come to cherish. Reminiscent of the time Marilyn had her stroke, I was again too busy to recognize her state of being. Oh, I knew something seemed wrong, but my hectic schedule hindered my ability to act on it. My intentions were good, but I neglected to elevate Marilyn to high-priority, taking for granted that she would patiently wait.

Just like anyone who comes to God wounded, Marilyn still had some complex issues that needed to be resolved. On many occasions she needed an ear to bend, a shoulder to cry on, and a counselor to advise her. Primarily, it was my responsibility to fulfill that role, yet I felt drained by the hours of conversation discussing the same problems—her health, her doubt, her troubled past—again and again. It wasn't her fault—I just felt frustrated with myself because I had run out of answers. I felt emotionally drained and perhaps avoided her to some extent.

Finally one night, I knew it was time to have a serious talk.

"You've got to tell me what's been wrong with you lately," I pleaded.

"I need you to sit down and make time for me!" she said, irritated. "For months I didn't say anything because I knew the pressure you were under with your brother and your dad dying, and I didn't want to push you; but you've had time for everybody else and you've forgotten about me!"

"I'm sorry! I'm trying to find time, but I've got work pulling me a hundred different directions, ministry at church, which is sometimes like having a second job, and then trying to teach Bible studies—not to mention trying to make time for family!" I said with rising frustration. "Sometimes I feel like I'm ready to lose my mind!" I cried.

Then Marilyn raised her voice, too.

"You said, when you bring somebody into the church, they are your spiritual children! Well, I'm your spiritual child—that makes you my spiritual parent! You're responsible for me and I need your help!

I know I bring the same problems to you every time—issues from my past, struggles with understanding how God works—and you give me the same answers; but sometimes I forget, and I just need to hear them over again until they stick in my mind!"

It was a stinging indictment against me—mainly, because she was right. For months now I had failed her. Because she was still a "babe in the Lord," I had committed the spiritual equivalent of "child neglect." I felt tremendous shame. In my zeal to share the gospel with as many people as possible, I had done so to the point of ignoring Marilyn. She loved the Bible study, and once it ended with the final lesson, she asked me to teach her more; but I had dropped the ball. I had declared her rock-solid in the faith, upgraded her to "maintenance" and moved on to the next prospect. I had placed her on solid foods when clearly she still needed the "milk" of the Word.

Not only that, but I had been ignorant of the fact that she hadn't been looking well lately—tired and worn down. I felt God's conviction provoking me to change my behavior. I also felt the devil's harsh condemnation. *Some soul winner you are! You let your offspring die of malnutrition! You let your fruit die on the vine!*

Marilyn's e-mail to her friends, Nancy and Daniel—

Dear Nancy and Daniel,

Thank you both for your silence. Thank you for not calling or writing. Thank you for letting me alone.

I can only put it this way…I'm tired.

I'm tired in every way that it's possible to be tired; physically, mentally, spiritually, emotionally, every way. I'm tired of taking care of everything and everybody, including myself, and doing it alone. I'm tired of trusting and believing people. I'm tired of caring. I'm tired of circumstances being what they are and I'm tired of not being able to see a silver lining anymore. I'm tired of myself for feeling sorry for myself. I'm tired of being told to count my blessings. I'm tired of trying to see other people's points of view. I'm tired of being acceptable only when I have on my happy face. I'm tired of reaching out and tired of resenting it when someone doesn't reach back. I'm tired of not being able to rise above the little things. I'm tired of having small hurts turn into big ones. I'm tired of crying. I'm tired of not knowing why I'm crying…

Love, Marilyn

None of the grievances listed in her e-mail to Nancy and Daniel were assigned to anyone in particular, but I knew better. I had been a significant part of Marilyn's life for almost three years now and had clearly been a source of joy for her. I would be foolish to think that I wouldn't also be responsible for at least some of her pain.

In one sense, it was a relief to know that our relationship had matured to the point that Marilyn could actually get mad at me. For a while I had wondered if her love for me bordered on idolatry. I cherished the love she had for me—the way she expressed it in word and deed—but I didn't want to be placed on a pedestal. The higher the pedestal, the more it would hurt getting knocked off.

And knocked off it, I was. I offered my sincerest apology to Marilyn for hurting her. It was the last thing I ever wanted to do to her. She, of course, accepted my apology, but I was going to have to make some changes in our relationship to prove I meant it—which I did.

At first she was a bit tentative, but eventually things improved. Fortunately, Joe and Katie's wedding was coming up in a few weeks and it would provide a great opportunity for family interaction and a much needed diversion from the heavy feelings we were both trying to dispatch.

I also apologized to God—for running from my responsibilities, for neglecting the very thing I had prayed so hard for, and for violating the trust God had placed in me. I wanted my problem to become an opportunity to learn from it.

Proverbs 11:30 says, *he that winneth souls is wise*. Most people believe that the scripture means a man is wise *for* winning souls to God, but I believe it also means he needs to be wise *so* he can win souls to God. Fact is, much of that wisdom is gained from the times we flat out blow it—but I'd rather fumble on occasion than to never have played in the game.

A few days later, I received a surprising phone call. Joe requested that I co-officiate his wedding ceremony. My heart was touched. For the last three years I had treaded lightly with Joe and David, searching for my proper place in their lives, not wanting to overstep my bounds. After all, it must have been bizarre for them to have me, a total stranger, suddenly burst upon the scene, especially considering the enormous amount of change it brought to their mother's life. Ever since we met, I went to great lengths to respect their feelings and try to remember how difficult the change must have been for them.

Joe's sincerity in asking me was genuine. He never once sounded forced or obligated to creatively "work me into" his special day. I truly felt wanted. It was a kind gesture and I counted it an honor to accept his request.

Marilyn's e-mail to her friend, Daniel—

...It's been ten days since Joe and Katie's wedding. It was a very nice wedding and everyone seemed to have a good time. I know I did. And Joe and Katie sure did. It was a time filled with family. For the second time in a month, my entire family was together, although it was too busy for any of them to spend much time with each other.

...The ceremony was very nice, too. They had chosen a church to have it in. They chose this particular church because it's a pretty church and because they really liked the pastor. They won't be joining this church, but they had to attend some pre-marriage classes with the pastor and they liked that.

Ed did the ring ceremony part of it. I was glad that Joe and Katie included him in that and, of course, Ed did a great job...he simply gave a very touching little lesson on the significance of the rings.

For the most part, life returned to normal after the wedding. When Marilyn and I had our falling out, one of the things I tried to explain to her was that she needed to utilize Pastor Yonts more, that some of her issues were becoming difficult for me to help her with because of my close relationship to her. It's not that I didn't want to listen, but I was having a hard time juggling the role of son, minister, and pastor.

At first the notion hurt her, as if she thought I was saying, *I can't help you any more, so I'm turning you over to somebody else*, which was certainly not the case. I simply knew that God endues a pastor with an anointing of wisdom that nobody else in the church receives, equipping him for the role of shepherd. But instead of feeling slighted, Marilyn heeded my advice, began to counsel more with Pastor Yonts, and found his guidance to be valuable and refreshing.

She also found an unexpected confidant in Evangelist Tim Greene, who was preaching an extended revival for our church. He and his family had been with us for over six weeks, and he made such an impression on Marilyn that she eventually had every one of his sermons copied onto cassette tape. Being less knowledgeable of her past and present situation, he was a great help in providing an objective opinion to her without any bias of facts . . .

Marilyn's e-mail to her friend, Daniel—

We've had a lot of things going on at church. That wonderful evangelist [Rev. Tim Greene] is still here, so we have services several times a week. His messages just blow me away. I've taken on some extra responsibilities at church, too, but that's where I want to put my energy these days. I've found a home there, Daniel, a sanctuary, a place I'm comfortable, and I don't just mean with the people who are there.

I love everything about this, the reading and studying and learning, the doctrine, the peace and excitement that I feel, both at the same time, and, most of all, the presence of God that simply overwhelms me at times and takes my breath away. I would have laughed at those words three years ago and I don't expect anyone else to understand what I mean, but it's the truth.

I'm feeling better now, too.

I've been sitting here for ten minutes trying to find words to explain that last sentence, but I can't seem to. I just feel better than before, better than I have for a long time. I might never be able to explain what happened to me, even to myself. I've come to terms with some things in my life and I'm working on others.

(((((((((((Fo meelon hugs and even more kisses)))))))))))

Love, Marilyn

In two months it would be the three year anniversary of the night we met. Sure, we had had some bumps in the road, some ups and some downs, but all in all, it had been an absolutely incredible journey together. Meeting Marilyn had been the catalyst for a wonderful, ongoing story—every year we were adding miracles, chapter by chapter. I simply couldn't imagine what God had in store for us next!

Chapter 11

November 2002
Menasha, Wisconsin

*M*y ringing cell phone jolted me out of a freeway-induced daydream. With Thanksgiving here in ten days, I was making a mad dash around the state. As a sales representative for a Connecticut-based company, I was attempting to see a few customers before they all went on vacation.

"Hello? This is Ed."

"Hi, do you have a minute or are you busy?" Marilyn's tinny voice blared through the speaker into the cab of my pickup truck.

"No, not busy at all." I said, "Just toolin' down the highway."

"Well, I wanted to ask you a question."

"Fire away."

"I want to call Shirley and ask her to do a Bible study with me on Tuesday nights, but I'm not sure how to start," Marilyn said. "She's been going to church for years, but I know there's something missing in her life. She reads and studies the Bible, and I'm afraid I don't know enough to teach her."

Marilyn and Shirley had been long-time acquaintances. As of late, their relationship was evolving into more of a friendship which started when Marilyn invited Shirley over to tell "the story." They shared the common experience of giving up a child for adoption, but for all the years they were casual friends, Shirley had never known that fact about Marilyn.

"Well, first of all, you don't need to feel intimidated—you know a lot more than you probably think you do," I encouraged. "Secondly, remember, God has revealed some things to you that have completely changed your life, and you now have a testimony.

You've had the same experiences happen to you that a person can read about in the Bible, and that's very powerful."

"I just want her to find what I've found," She said, plaintively.

"I know you do. That's a heart of compassion speaking and that only comes from the Holy Ghost," I told her. "I say, just grab your Bible study chart and manual and start preparing. When you call her, don't offer to 'teach' her—just offer to get together as friends and the open door will be there."

"Alright, that's what I'll do," Marilyn said. "Oh, by the way, don't make any plans for Saturday, December seventh. You know what that is, right?"

"Yes, I certainly do…"

"I want to have you, Paula and the kids over for dinner, okay?"

"I wouldn't dare plan anything else," I said teasingly.

It would be the eve of our three year anniversary of the first night we met.

I hung up feeling so blessed and proud. Marilyn was taking the next step in her walk with God—reaching out to others—and becoming a soul winner. The next day Marilyn called Shirley. They set their first study for the Tuesday after Thanksgiving.

It was one of those times a preacher dreads. I sought the mind of God for the Sunday morning service I was to preach five days before Thanksgiving, but nothing would come. I toiled at the computer, the Bible, and in prayer, but my mind kept going back to the sermon on Job I preached five months before—the one I never intended to preach again: *In All This, Yet Will I Praise Him!*

A part of me felt like I was copping out. *Lord, it's too easy to pull out a sermon I've preached before in another church and use it here at home. It's not fresh bread!* But the compulsion only grew, until by Sunday morning, I was convinced this was what the Lord intended for me to preach.

As is usual for me, the sermon came out slightly different than the first time, but just as passionate. The response from the congregation was fine, but I didn't feel the Spirit of God drawing me to anyone in particular as I preached. I couldn't help wondering who the message was for, specifically. I trusted that God knew who needed to hear it. That is better left in the hands of the Lord—I do the "people stuff," He does the "God stuff."

After church, Paula, the kids and I went to lunch with Marilyn and Shirley. "I've got a project to do!" Marilyn announced excitedly, while we were waiting for our food to come.

"And what's that?" Paula asked, smiling.

"I was in one of my internet forums yesterday, and the subject that came up was: *'What is your favorite day?'* Marilyn explained, "Of course, I said 'Sundays.' Then they asked me 'Why?' I didn't want to just give them a quick answer so I said I would work on it and then post it later for them to read."

"Ooo, that ought to be fun," Paula said. "Make sure you give me a copy when you're done!"

Before we knew it, another Thanksgiving was upon us. The year had been bittersweet—joy and heartache had merged onto the road of life we traveled, but thankfulness was still in order. For me, it would be the first time that my dad would not be with us for the Thanksgiving gathering at my Great-Aunt Phyllis' house. For Marilyn, this would be her first without her brother, Steve, but Eli would be at her house where preparations were now being made to feed a small army of family members who would gather to give thanks. Another reason for Marilyn to be thankful: Joe and Katie were expecting!

"Ed, do you think you would have some time to come over and get my roaster from the basement and bring it upstairs for me?" Marilyn asked me a week before Thanksgiving. "It doesn't have to be right away, just sometime before Wednesday night."

"Sure, that'd be no problem."

A couple of nights before she was to have guests, I stopped by the house to retrieve the roaster and some extra folding chairs from the basement. I was concerned about how she was feeling. Marilyn seemed to be fighting the flu-bug for about two weeks and it was relentless, draining her of energy. She just hadn't been herself. After I was finished downstairs, we stopped to talk.

"Are you going to be alright with all this cooking and people coming over?" I asked, studying her closely after noticing all the ingredients piled high on the countertops.

"I'll be fine," she assured me. "I'll have plenty of help when everyone gets here."

As usual, it had been a busy few weeks for both of us, and so we hadn't had much chance to chat with each other. It was my intent to do my chore for her and then be on my way, but I found myself lingering, eager to talk for awhile.

"You know, I watched you with the boys the other night—you're so good with them," Marilyn said, as we stood in the entryway between the kitchen and living room. "They really do adore you."

"Well, thank you for saying that," I said, feeling self-conscious.

"I mean it, Ed, you really are a good father."

"Thank you," I whispered in her ear as we hugged each other.

We spent a few more minutes together, but then I needed to get back home because it was getting late. Walking out the door, I told her we would stop over on Thanksgiving evening after we got back into town.

Thursday, November 28, 2002
Thanksgiving Day

"I'll call to make sure it's not too late for us to stop by," Paula said, dialing the cell phone on our way back to Appleton. I listened to the one-sided conversation.

"Hi, Carol? . . . Hi, this is Paula . . . Happy Thanksgiving to you, too. Is Marilyn there? . . . *Sleeping?* Is she feeling okay? . . . Okay, well, we're heading back to town. Are you all going to be staying longer so we can come by and say 'Hi?' . . . Okay, great! We'll see you in a little bit then."

"So, what's going on?" I asked after she hung up.

"Carol said Marilyn wasn't feeling well and was really tired, so she went to lay down with Eli to take a nap."

"Should we even go over there? It's getting late, anyway."

"Sure, it's not that late. They're all still going to be there, and I know Marilyn would want us to stop by to see everybody."

Marilyn was up when we arrived and, sure enough, the house was still full. It looked like it had been a long day for her, so we didn't plan to stay very long. It looked like the flu had continued to take its toll on her. We visited with everyone for about an hour and then packed up to go—tomorrow was going to be a busy day. Jordan was singing with the *Appleton Boychoir* for the grand opening of the new, twenty-five hundred seat, *Fox Cities Performing Arts Center* in downtown Appleton and we all had tickets to go.

Friday, November 29, 2002

Marilyn still seemed tired the next day, so she rode with David and Suzette in their car, and Paula and I took the kids in ours. We all met in the lobby of the *Performing Arts Center* to go up to our fourth level seats as a group of twelve. Marilyn and I sat next to each other in the row behind most of the others. The Appleton Boychoir sang before a packed house and performed beautifully. We were so proud of Jordan! Marilyn brought her opera glasses and we took turns watching him—he looked so composed.

The headlining performance was anticlimactic, not to mention, quite strange. It was written by some supposedly well-known person in the artistic world of playwrights. I guess only highly-cultured folks appreciate the kind of performance we witnessed. Frankly, Marilyn and I were bored to tears, as were most other people around us, some choosing to leave early.

We had more fun laughing and whispering, swapping irreverent comments back and forth between us like two naughty children. The target of our cheeky banter was the lead actor, named Blue Meanie, and his robin-egg-blue tights! People's smiling faces occasionally turned our way to get in on our impertinence in hopes of relieving their own boredom.

Our snickers died down only after we ran out of one-liners and resigned ourselves to having to endure the performance to the bitter end. We finally went back to chatting quietly and holding hands as we had been, on and off, all evening.

It was late by the time we got back down to the lobby. Everyone was tired, so we hugged, said our good-byes and made plans for Marilyn, Suzette and Eli to come over in the morning for breakfast.

Marilyn was physically worn out and needed assistance from Suzette, in the form of an arm to lean on, so she could cross the street to head to the parking ramp.

Saturday, November 30, 2002...the three year anniversary of the phone call that led to our meeting

It was sunny in the morning but the temperature had dropped. Once everybody got into the house, we swapped "anniversary" hugs and then gathered in the kitchen for pancakes. (There's something wonderfully cozy about family crowding around the table in a toasty-warm kitchen on a cold day.)

Paula, who is known for making exceptional coffee, cranked up the espresso machine and served hazelnut and vanilla lattes to Marilyn and Suzette, shortly thereafter. Jordan and Jonathan found a foam ball and were playing "catch" with Eli in the living room. In addition to his throw, Eli was working on his favorite word, *baaw-l*, a two syllable enunciation, the latter rising sharply in his high-pitch baby-boy voice.

I offered to cook, daring to show myself in the kitchen before wrestling with an extreme case of "bad hair." Considering how short my hair is, I never cease to amaze myself—and others—with the purely artistic creations I'm able to form after an eight-hour snooze.

Once my vanity had been cast to the wind, dignity soon followed. In between flipping pancakes, I commenced to performing some of rock-n-roll's most beloved Elvis songs—using the spatula as a microphone—complete with sleepy eyes, quivering upper lip, arm gesticulations, and a whole lot of *"Thank you, thank you very much,"* (Gyrating hips, however, were not included).

Suzette had a busy day coming up on Sunday and needed to get on the road for her two-hour drive home with Eli, so we all congregated by the back door as the three of them bundled up, preparing to leave. Marilyn stood in front of me, looking into my eyes while the others around us exchanged "Goodbye" hugs.

"Happy Anniversary," she said.

"Happy Anniversary," I replied, reaching out to hug her.

Marilyn squeezed me tight for a long moment. Before completely withdrawing, she began to kiss my cheek in staccato fashion—mmmmah! . . . mmmmah! . . . mmmmah! . . . mmmmah! When she was finished I grinned at her affectionately, shaking my head at her unrestrained display of love.

"I love you, Ed."

"I love you, too."

Later in the evening, Marilyn and Paula had tickets to see the enchanting story of Cinderella at the Weidner Center in Green Bay. The annual holiday excursion was a tradition Marilyn had been carrying on for years with her long-time friends, Kathy and Kaye. After Marilyn had introduced Paula to them, they had invited Paula to join their yearly night out. Tonight would be Paula's third year in a row going.

Initially, they planned to go out to eat, but Marilyn had asked to skip dinner because she wasn't up to it—concerned that she might tire out if the night went too long. Later that evening Paula picked Marilyn up at her house and drove to Green Bay.

"Do you think you could drop me off at the door?" Marilyn asked as Paula turned into the parking lot.

"Hey, why don't we splurge and do valet parking?" Paula suggested.

"Sounds good to me," Marilyn said. "I'll pay half!"

. The performance was as humorous as it was charming. Marilyn and Paula laughed together and chatted back and forth under their breath throughout the night. When the curtain finally fell, it was getting late. Bidding good-night to Kathy and Kaye, they had the valet retrieve the car and then began the forty minute drive home, reminiscing the whole way about all the miracles that God had done in the past three years.

"I've got the munchies!" Paula hinted as they were pulling into Marilyn's driveway.

"Why don't you do me a big favor and come in and help me polish off some of these Thanksgiving leftovers?" Marilyn suggested.

"Okay, sounds good to me."

They picked up where their conversation had left off in the car, while Marilyn sat at the kitchen table and Paula fixed turkey sandwiches. They talked for another hour, sentimentally recalling the events of the past three years. Now it was late. In another hour it would be exactly one week until the three year anniversary of the night we first met.

"This is the most I've eaten in a while," Marilyn commented, surprised by an appetite that had been absent for weeks.

"You know, I haven't been real worried about you because it took me two weeks to get over the flu, and you've been having the same symptoms; but since everybody else is so concerned about you, it's making me worried," Paula said. "You have a lot of people who love you and care about you. You really should go see a doctor."

"This is the best I've felt in a while, but if I don't continue to feel better, I'll go to the doctor on Monday," Marilyn assured her.

How appropriate that on the day marking the anniversary of the phone call that began our real-life fairy tale, Paula and Marilyn would end that night with a fairy tale. Like Cinderella, Marilyn had overcome a life of practical existence, overshadowed by an unpleasant secret, which for years was hidden from view to the outside world.

It took the magical meeting of an unknown, but well- connected, relative with a compassionate understanding of her need to introduce her to royalty—in this case, *the Prince of Peace*. This Prince would ultimately make her His bride—the betrothal coming in the form of taking His name in baptism and the receiving of His Spirit— bestowing upon her the promise of life—and life more abundant— the blessings of His kingdom, and the riches of His glory.

After all, doesn't every fairy tale have a happy ending?

Sunday, December 1, 2002

The bedside phone startled us, ringing just past six o'clock in the morning. Suddenly aware of how early it was, Paula came alive quickly and reached for the handset next to her. It was still dark outside.

"Hello?" she answered groggily. "What's the matter? . . . uh, huh. Okay. . ."

I was having a hard time waking up because I wasn't able to sleep until Paula had gotten home safely the night before—then we talked till well past midnight. I could tell it was Marilyn on the line, so my early-morning fog was quickly clearing as I listened to the uneasiness in Paula's voice.

"Do you want Ed to come over, too? . . . Okay . . . Do you want him to pray with you? . . . Okay, just a second."

By now I was sitting up, frowning with concern, anxiously wanting to know what was wrong. Paula cupped her hand over the phone and pulled it away from her mouth.

"She says she doesn't feel good—her heart's racing!" Paula whispered with urgency. I grabbed the phone from her.

"Hey, what's going on?" I said calmly, attempting to mask my growing concern.

"I don't know. My heart's racing and I don't feel well," Marilyn repeated to me.

"When did all this start?"

"I woke up feeling this way so I called Joe. He's on his way over now to take me to the hospital."

"Okay, just try to relax and let's pray together, okay?"

"Alright."

"Lord, I'm asking, by the power and authority of the Name of Jesus, that you touch Marilyn in her body, right now," I prayed into the phone. "You know what the problem is and you have the ability to make it right. Take dominion over this illness, in Jesus' Name. I'm asking you to help Marilyn relax and be confident that everything will be okay. I pray that a spirit of peace would come upon her and a knowledge that she is in Your hands. I plead the blood of Jesus over her! In Jesus' Name! Amen."

"Amen," she whispered into the phone.

"I'll be right over," I assured her.

"Please, hurry!"

I swiftly jumped out of bed, gathered my clothes and darted into the bathroom to get ready as fast as possible.

"Just in case this is serious, I'm going to call her back and keep her on the phone until you get over there," Paula called out from the bedroom a moment later.

"Yeah, okay," I shouted back.

She quickly punched in the number and waited. The phone continued to ring until finally Marilyn's voice came over the answering machine. *Hi, I'm not able to take your call right now . . .*

"Ed, she's not answering!"

Punching redial, Paula tensely waited again. After a few rings, the phone was picked up abruptly.

"I gotta call 911! My mom's lying on the floor unconscious!" Joe said frantically, immediately hanging up.

I was just about ready when Paula shouted to me.

"Joe answered—he found her unconscious!" Paula called out. "He's calling 911, right now!"

I raced out the door and jumped into my truck. Throwing the shifter into drive, I squealed the tires trying to get to her house as quickly as possible.

Driving fast through the quiet streets, I again experienced the surreal sensation of acting a part in a dream—one in which I was helpless to control the outcome of what was happening—like I had just six months earlier on my way to the hospital to see my dad. It was a dream in which I found myself immersed in a foreboding sense of impending tragedy.

There was one small exception. This time, I knew that the measuring stick of my faith was not in what the outcome would be after I prayed, but in my ability to trust and acknowledge God's sovereignty and His promise that all things work together for good to them that love Him. So I prayed as I drove: *Jesus, be with her, watch over her—and let Your will be done.*

Just before cresting the overpass that spans the freeway bypass a block from Marilyn's house, I prepared myself to see the early morning darkness pierced by flashing red and blue emergency lights. Seeing them, just as I had pictured I would, brought me one step closer from surreal to very real. I whipped in front of the ambulance parked in the street and slammed the shifter into park. The sky was overcast, but the sun must have broken over the hidden horizon because it suddenly seemed lighter than it was during the drive over. Small flakes of snow began to fall as I got out of the truck, covering the frozen, brown grass in the yard.

Katie was standing outside talking on her cell phone. She was scared and crying. She interrupted her conversation as we hugged tightly. The front storm door was hanging wide open, drifting lazily in the breeze; the screws attaching the door closer to the doorframe were torn out of their holes, apparently from the emergency workers urgency to get in the house.

Leaving Katie outside, I went into the house. The furniture in the living room was in disarray, having been shoved aside hastily to make room for the emergency medical workers—more people than seemed able to fit in the small space. My eyes adjusted to see the kitchen alive with intense activity, a cacophony of unfamiliar sounds filling the entire apartment. There, in the midst of frantic emergency workers kneeling all around her, lay Marilyn's prostrate form.

Through the din I spotted Joe across the room. I motioned urgently for him to come over. He jockeyed back and forth, looking like a caged lion searching for an opening to squeeze through. Eventually we got squeezed down the hallway where the bedrooms were located.

"What's going on?" I asked, my hands shaking.

"I got here and found her on the floor. Then the phone rang . . ."

He was interrupted by a police officer asking if we knew of any medications Marilyn was on, and if so, where were they might be located. Katie then joined us and we all began to frantically search the bedroom and bathroom, looking for prescription bottles. We stopped looking after not finding anything in the drawers and cabinets. To combat the helpless feeling, I had an urgent desire to pray. I summoned Joe and Katie.

"Guys, I don't know what your belief in God is," I stammered, my voice quaking from the strain, "but I believe the only thing we can do right now to help Marilyn is to pray." They both nodded their heads. We formed a circle and held hands.

We no sooner had begun to pray, then another officer interrupted us, asking our names and relationship to Marilyn. I immediately recognized him as the officer that had been the police liaison at my junior high school over 20 years ago when I got in trouble for underage drinking. (Strange are the thoughts that course through your mind with such clarity in times of extreme stress!) When I gave him my name and said I was Marilyn's son, I suddenly wondered if he might have recognized me and been confused—he had also been on the police force with my dad.

We were now stuck in Marilyn's bedroom because the kitchen and hallway were unable to support any more people. We could not see what was going on—only hear the sound of muffled voices, the scraping of shoes across the linoleum floor, and a strange mixture of unidentifiable noises emanating from the kitchen, echoing down the hallway.

As I was speaking to the police officer, I became increasingly more aware of a loud crashing sound coming from the kitchen, vibrating through the floor of the house. I briefly pictured somebody lifting up a kitchen chair into the air and slamming it down onto the floor. Later I realized it was the sound of the stretcher being urgently hauled into the house. A hauntingly eerie, low-pitched moaning reverberated in my ears from the air escaping through the bag valve mask used to force oxygen into Marilyn's now-still lungs.

We were finally able to leave the back bedroom, once the paramedics were prepared to load Marilyn into the ambulance. I noticed her bare feet sticking out from under the blanket, making me conscious of how cold and damp it had become since the light dusting of snow began falling. I was further saddened by the fact that her slippers now lay on the kitchen floor next to where she collapsed.

Joe and Katie left in their car to get a head start to the hospital. I climbed in my truck and waited for the ambulance to pass me before pulling out to follow it to the hospital.

It was still early in the morning, and the ambulance was leaving tire tracks in the fresh snow—mesmerizing me as I trailed behind. While in the truck, I called Paula to tell her to meet me at the emergency room. She was desperate to know how Marilyn was doing, but I wanted to be face-to-face when I told her everything I had witnessed.

Immediately, Paula called some friends from church to request a prayer-chain be started and then jumped into her van. Ten minutes later, when I pulled into the parking lot of the hospital, she was waiting for me.

"How is she?" Paula asked warily, looking directly into my face, searching to find a ray of hope in my expression.

"I don't think she's going to make it," I said simply, looking down. Numbly, we embraced for a few minutes in the parking lot and then made our way through the swooshing sound of the parting automatic doors leading into the emergency room.

A nurse directed us to a small waiting room for families—similar to the one I had been in recently—informing us that doctors were working on Marilyn and that one of them would be in soon to talk with us. As we waited for an update, Joe called David, who lived almost two hours away, to inform him of what was happening and to request that he get to the hospital as soon as possible.

A few minutes later, Danny Sharp, my assistant pastor, appeared in the doorway and knocked lightly. He introduced himself to those that didn't know him and asked permission to pray with us. Heads around the room nodded in concurrence. Many joined hands in unity and the spirit of faith as he lifted his voice and began to pray.

Tears were now beginning to fall and hugs were being exchanged, as the muted sound of soft voices filtered through the room. With David now on his way, there was nothing to do but pray. After a short wait, a doctor in light-blue hospital scrubs filled the doorway. He introduced himself, addressing the entire group. A nurse with an uneasy look on her face lingered close behind.

"We tried everything possible," he said with compassionate eyes, "I'm sorry—your mother didn't make it."

The air left the room.

Chapter 12

*T*here was a long, silent pause before anyone moved. We allowed the words to resonate through our minds for a moment so we could begin the process of accepting the harshest of truths. Our hearts would have to come around much later. The stunning blow was simple: Marilyn was gone—the fairy tale was over. Gone were our plans for the future. Gone was our eager anticipation for the next chapter of this amazing story to be lived out.

The author, Louis L'Amour, once said: *A body shouldn't heed what might be. He's got to do with what is.* In the course of a few brief moments, what might have been, disappeared, leaving behind what was—a bottomless chasm of heartbreak and an endless abyss of disbelief. It caused me to reflect back on an e-mail she had written shortly after her stroke . . .

Marilyn's e-mail to her friend, Daniel—

...The realization of seeing a lot of Ed in me brings a little pain though...actually, more regret than pain. I wish I could have seen him grow up, been there with him, watched him become the person he is. It's a sense of time lost. It's not that I dwell on that, but it becomes more acute when I think about what's happening to me now...

It's a sense of time running out and please don't think I'm being morbid about that. It's true for everyone, but I've been slapped with a clear reminder in the last few weeks [after having her stroke]. I guess what I'm saying is that...whatever time he and I have left together isn't going to be enough for either of us. Those missing 35 years...

For what is your life? It is even a vapor that appeareth for a little time, and then vanisheth away.

Every life we come in contact with affects us in some way. Some we view from afar, purely observing, as if watching a rolling bank of fog in the distance—driven along on the wings of the wind. Some lives we only touch at the edges, theirs drifting in and out of ours with the recurrent change of atmosphere. And then, there are some that completely overwhelm us.

For three years Marilyn's life surrounded me like a cloud—her vapor engulfing me. Every direction I turned, I could see her—sense her—she was there. Her life did not merely touch me, it enveloped me. This vapor was different than any other in my life—I was part of it. I came from it.

And when it vanished away, a part of me faded with it.

Nobody wanted to speak the obvious—the proper time would come later—but all who were aware of Marilyn not feeling well for the past two weeks were thinking the same thing: *We missed it! She had been in the midst of heart failure and we missed it!* Only now did we understand how seriously ill she had been.

People began to stand up and look around for the nearest person to console. Making my way around the room, I came to stand in front of Joe. We reached out to each other in a tight embrace.

"I'm *so* sorry, Joe."

"I'm sorry, too."

The room became claustrophobic, forcing people to spill out into the hallway *en masse* to await David's arrival. I slowly made my way toward the emergency room entrance and spotted my close friends, Bill and Lynn coming through the door. As Bill walked up to me, it was obvious how deeply concerned he and Lynn were. They were extremely devoted to Marilyn, many times inviting her out to their house.

It's a peaceful haven, which sits high upon on a hill overlooking Lake Winnebago, where the stresses of life seem to disappear. Marilyn loved it at Bill and Lynn's, as does anybody privileged enough to be invited out for an evening of their warm, rural hospitality.

"Do you know what's going on?" Bill asked, anxiously. "Is she alright?" I was momentarily confused by his words until I realized, *He doesn't know!*

"Nobody told you? Bill, she didn't make it—she's gone."

"*No!* . . . Oh, Ed. I'm *so* sorry," Bill said, squeezing me tightly, his face now soaking wet with tears as he wept unashamedly. I fought back the rising lump in my throat, afraid that if I let go of my emotions here and now, I might not recover them.

Word was spreading quickly. A few minutes later my friend, Jeff, walked in. I wasn't surprised. He had been there for me through the loss of my father and brother, his friendship precious and priceless.

After him, Pastor Yonts came. His was a comforting and reassuring presence that only a shepherd can bring to a tragic situation.

Finally, a blue compact car pulled in swiftly under the overhang, braking to a sudden stop. There was a collective breath held by everyone as Joe went out to meet David. I watched through the glass doors as David got out of the car. Standing in front of Joe, he listened for a moment. Suddenly David wrapped his arms around his brother in a long, tight embrace. I had to turn away.

Another round of tears and hugs started as soon as David, Suzette, and Eli came in from outside. We requested of the nurse some time to go back and see Marilyn. Joe and Katie went first, rejoining us a few minutes later in the waiting area, their faces wet. David, Suzette and Eli went next, coming back looking the same. My stomach felt heavy as Paula and I steeled ourselves against the impending pain we were about to feel.

The nurses had done a fine job preparing her. Marilyn lay there looking peaceful with no outward sign of the ordeal her body had just gone through. Her hand was positioned across her body ready to be held. It was quiet all around us as we stood on each side of her. We spoke very few words. I simply took her hand and whispered the first thing that came to my mind—*thank you.*

There were practical considerations that now needed to be discussed between myself, Joe and David. Because of my status as brother-come-lately, I was still uncertain of my position in their eyes. Yet, when it came time to talk about what should be done next, they included me totally, without hesitation. Joe, David and I went back to the small family room, closed the door, and sat down facing each other. Our relationship was about to start a new chapter. Joe spoke first.

"I haven't really understood all the changes in Mom's life. Since she met you and Paula, she's been so different," he began. "It's like we had two mothers—the one we grew up with and the one we've known the last three years." David was silent, nodding his head in agreement.

"But I will say this," Joe continued, "I've never seen her happier at any time in her life."

"Guys," I began hesitantly, "I know it's been hard for you to understand all that's happened to her, but I need to tell you something. There's no doubt that meeting Paula and me had an effect on Marilyn—I acknowledge that fact—but the profound change in her personality and the happiness that you've seen was not because of us; it was because of her relationship with God. Marilyn discovered that God is real. That's why she was so different."

(Even if they couldn't comprehend what I just said, I wanted them to know that my role was minor compared to what Jesus Christ did for their mother and that the credit properly belonged to Him.)

"I want to thank both of you for sharing your mom with me. I was a stranger that suddenly entered your lives," I said. "You didn't have to accept me, especially being that I'm so different, but you did—and I thank you very much for that."

"Well, you're still our brother," David affirmed while Joe nodded his head in agreement. "We're *all* different but we still share the same blood."

The lump in my throat was back.

Twenty minutes later, we left the room agreeing that the visitation should be held at the same funeral home where Danny had been shown five years and one month ago, nearly to the day. We also decided, per Joe's suggestion, that the funeral be held at my church—or rather, Marilyn's church—with Pastor Yonts officiating.

While the three of us were meeting in the family room, Bill and Lynn were with Paula in the waiting area.

"Are we Apostolic or not?" Bill asked resolutely.

"I was thinking the same thing," Paula said.

"Has anybody prayed for her?"

"I don't think so."

They informed the nurse that they would like to see Marilyn again and then asked for some privacy. Laying their hands on Marilyn they began to pray: *Lord, you put breath in her body once before, you can do it again . . .*

When they finished praying, Paula looked up with a tear-stained face and said, "Bill, do you really think she would want to come back?"

"No, probably not," he replied, slowly shaking his head.

We all left the hospital, agreeing to spend the evening together as a family at Joe and Katie's house. It was hard to believe, after all that had happened already, that it was still early in the morning, and the ten o'clock church service hadn't begun yet.

Emotionally, Paula and I were stretched thin. As much as I needed to be in the presence of God at Sunday service, I couldn't bring myself to look into the sad faces of our church family so soon after absorbing this shock. Besides, we had one more heart-wrenching task ahead of us at home—informing Jordan and Jonathan that they had lost another grandparent.

They took the news hard—it was the third time in a year and a half that I sat them down on the couch to tell them that a family member had died.

We had been home only a short time when the doorbell rang. Paula opened the door to find Shirley standing there on the verge of tears. After receiving the news by phone from a friend, she went to the church, hoping we would be there. Not finding us, she immediately drove to our house a few blocks away.

Shirley took a seat on the couch in the exact spot that Marilyn sat the first night we met. She talked, cried and grieved over what might have been in her new-found relationship with Marilyn.

"Did you know that we were going to be starting a Bible study together this Tuesday?" Shirley asked.

"Yes, Marilyn told us that," Paula said.

"I was really looking forward to that," Shirley lamented.

"I know," I replied. "Marilyn was, too."

On Monday morning, David, Joe and Katie, and Paula and I went to begin making the funeral arrangements. We left the bank after having opened Marilyn's safe deposit box and retrieving her personal documents. From there we went to the funeral home.

The director, Tim, remembered Marilyn from when Danny had passed away five years before. He also remembered Joe and David, which made for an interesting introduction of me as a brother! Tim's raised eyebrows and stutter only lasted for a moment until Joe explained not only *who* I was but *how* I came to be in their lives. Once that was clarified, we were ready to begin drafting the obituary.

"Okay, next we will list the children from eldest to youngest," Tim said when he got to the part about survivors. "We'll start with you, Joe. How do you want your name listed, Joe or Joseph?"

"Actually, Ed would be listed first," Joe replied.

"Yeah, first Ed, then Joe, then me," David added.

I was dumbstruck.

"Guys, I . . . um, you don't have to put me . . ." I said, fumbling for the right words, feeling like an interloper. Before I could finish, both of them started speaking at once.

"No, no. You're the oldest. That's the way it is and that's how we should list our names."

"Well, guys, I don't know what to say. Thank you," I said, struggling to express how moved I was by their insistence.

It was at that precise moment that I realized I had truly gained two brothers. Marilyn would have been overjoyed.

Wednesday, December 4, 2002

Church service had been called off the Wednesday night of the visitation. Most of the congregation, along with the ministerial staff, planned to be at the visitation, so there wasn't much point in opening the doors of the church.

We arrived at the funeral home just before visitation hours started—me and Paula, Joe and Katie, and David, Suzette and Eli.

Individually we began emotionally preparing ourselves to enter the room where Marilyn was being shown. With a deep breath, we walked in a few at a time, approaching the casket like one gets into a pool of cool water—slowly, gradually, trying to get used to the feel of it.

Being one of the last people to go in, I noticed people paired up in couples or families—all except Carol, Marilyn's sister, who was there by herself. My heart went out to her. Overshadowed by my own loss, I neglected to appreciate that Carol was now the only one of her immediate family left, having lost Steve ten months ago and now, Marilyn. I walked up next to her, put my arm around her shoulders and hugged her tight as we walked together toward the casket.

Marilyn looked beautiful. Her face was radiant, portraying a look of peace and serenity. Step by step, Carol and I drew near, but before we got to where Marilyn lay, I was forced to excuse myself as three days of pent-up emotion threatened to overwhelm me.

Transitioning from the shocked stage into acceptance, I found an empty room across the hall, sat down in a chair next to a window that looked out over the street, and began to sob, until Paula found me twenty minutes later. Together, we wept.

Daniel and Nancy arrived. They both had flown in to Chicago and drove up to Appleton together. They would stay with Joe and Katie for the rest of the week while David, Suzette and Eli stayed with us.

The visitation was scheduled from four o'clock to eight o'clock. People began to show up immediately. It was an increasingly steady flow all night until the crowded room could not contain them any longer. People spilled out into the foyer, as they stood in line to sign the attendance book, awaiting their chance to file past the casket. It was a busy night, as more than three hundred people came to pay their respects.

There were some that didn't know who I was, but more that did. Whether they knew "the story" previously or not, many were anxious to talk to me and Paula about our relationship with Marilyn. All night long I fielded the reoccurring question, phrased slightly different each time: "Don't you feel like you've been cheated since you only got three years with Marilyn?"

I found myself replying automatically.

"No. I don't feel cheated, I feel blessed. God gave me the last three years of her life—a window of opportunity—to know her and to share the gospel with her. I'm not angry. I'm only thankful."

Thursday, December 5, 2002

There was a crisp chill in the air as the sun broke the horizon, climbing into a cloudless sky and penetrating the cold by spreading its golden rays over the house. The emotionally taxing evening had left everyone lethargic and slow to get up—notwithstanding the fact that no one was in a hurry for one o'clock to come—the time of the funeral.

It had been my intention to not speak at the service—I didn't trust my ability to keep my emotions in check—but now I felt a sudden and desperate urge to write. While the house was awakening, I sat at the computer, able to order my thoughts for the first time in four days. We then got ready.

As one o'clock neared, the church was full to its capacity of 325. We lined up in the foyer, getting ready to enter the sanctuary in order of age. As was the case at the funeral home, Joe and David insisted on me, Paula and the boys going first. We walked to the casket, paid our last respects and then walked back to the foyer for the closing of the casket. After that was done, we came back into the sanctuary and were seated on the front row pew.

From the moment the service started there was a tender and sweet presence of God throughout the place. Pastor Yonts and Pastor Sharp opened the service with scripture and prayer. Pastor Yonts' wife, Lori sang; Marilyn's long-time friend, Laura, sang; Suzette sang; and those of us who chose to do so—myself, Paula, Daniel, David and Suzette—each spoke.

Everyone's message was different and beautiful, reflecting what Marilyn meant to each in a personal way. But Daniel's broke the ice. He so endeared himself to the people with his humor, that it prompted a standing ovation when he finished. It's the first time I've ever witnessed anything like it at a memorial service.

When I was summoned forward, I could feel God's strength buttressing me. Of the hundreds of times I stood behind this pulpit to lead worship or to preach, never had it been for anything like this. I held a letter to Marilyn in my hand—much like the one I first wrote to her before we met—except that this letter she would not be able to read. It was really for my own benefit, but I thought it appropriate that our relationship should end the same as it started . . .

My Dearest Marilyn:

"Thank you." Those were the first two words I ever communicated to you.

The night we first met I told you that I am here today because of the right choice you made so many years ago. I remember you replied, "For me there never was a choice whether or not to have you." But I believe there was.

People every day compromise their principles and convictions and beliefs due to the weight of stress. While under duress, they make decisions that alter the future, while the lives of others hang in the balance. You didn't compromise even when it would have been easy to do so.

Because of your decision, I have lived. Because of you my parents were able to realize their dream of adopting a child (although, I must say, there were times when I'm sure I made it seem more like a nightmare than a dream).

Because of you I had the opportunity to meet Paula, who is more than my wife; she's the best friend I have in the world. And because of her I have two of the most precious boys God has ever blessed a couple with.

I told you that during the years I grew up, I always had a vague mental picture of you but I couldn't see your face. Nonetheless, I loved you and respected you, even before I knew you.

Some might ask, "How is it possible to love someone you don't know?" For me the answer is simple: you gave me life. There is no way for me to verbalize the depth of gratitude I have in my heart.

Over the last three years we have often referred to our relationship as a fairy tale story—one fit for the Reader's Digest or a full length feature film. I remember talking about how we were continually adding chapters to the book and that someday you wanted to be the one to write it down so others would be blessed by the miracle. And, oh, what a three years it's been! We've packed a lot of love in that short amount of time.

Some might say this beautiful novel, with so many chapters left to write, was turned into a short story with a tragic ending. On the contrary, the miracle has just begun. The body that failed you is no longer holding you back and the pain and heartaches you struggled with are a distant memory. Like the Word of God says, No more pain, no more sorrow, for the former things are passed away. Remember our first few Bible studies when you struggled with how a person could believe in a God they couldn't see? Well, now you know.

You're in the arms of a gentle and loving Savior. You've discovered what II Corinthians 4:17, 18 says: For our light affliction, which is but for a moment, worketh for us a far more exceeding and eternal weight of glory; While we look not at the things which are seen, but at the things which are not seen: for the things which are seen are temporal; but the things which are not seen are eternal.

Oh, by the way, you'll need to forgive my little bit of jealousy. After all, before we met you didn't believe God even existed. Then I introduce you to Jesus and you go run off with Him right away.

Seriously though, I rejoice for you today. You've gone where my heart longs to be. But one day I know we shall be reunited, dancing together before the throne in worship, writing those unwritten chapters for eternity.

As for myself, the one who is left; well, don't fret for me. Remember that sermon I preached one week before you left us? Pretty ironic, isn't it? Well, I just want you to know that I still believe it as hard as I preached it that morning. Like Job, my mantel is rent and my head is shaved in mourning, but blessed be the Name of the Lord. Through all the heartache I still praise God. After all, how could I possibly curse God or charge Him foolishly? He's given me you for three wonderful years. He's strengthening me in my loss and is turning my mourning into dancing. Though the weeping has endured for a night, His joy has come in the morning. What I guess I'm trying to say is this; don't worry. Even though my heart's broken, I haven't forgotten the title of that sermon; In All This, Yet Will I Praise Him!

Marilyn, you haven't just touched my life, you've permeated every area of it. Birth mother and friend—words that are true but just can't capture the essence of what you've been to me. Even Daniel Webster would have had trouble finding the right word to describe it. But none of that really matters. What matters is that you just know how very much I love you and how deeply I will miss you. You've given me so much. You're gone but you've left for me a multitude of memories, a history of my past, and two terrific brothers who I am growing to love very much. You've blessed me beyond words.

And so I'll end my last letter to you just like I started the first, by simply saying, thank you.

Your loving son, Ed

Paula then stood at the podium to address the mourners after me, and began to explain the sentence written at the bottom of Marilyn's obituary.

After going out to lunch the Sunday before she died, Marilyn went home and wrote her response to the internet forum question, "What is your favorite day and Why?" Before leaving for church later that afternoon, she e-mailed it to Daniel but never posted it to the website. Once learning of her death, Daniel then forwarded the e-mail to Paula, who was deeply touched by what it said. Because of what Marilyn wrote, we placed the small sentence, all by itself, at the bottom of her obituary. It simply read, *"I Love Sundays."*

Paula then read the e-mail Marilyn had written to Daniel . . .

Hello, Daniel,

I have a few minutes to spare before I go back to church and it occurred to me that I really WOULD like to tell someone why I love Sundays.

Today was a typical Sunday in some ways, better than typical in others. It was a good day.

I love going to church, as you know. I love everything about it. I wish we had church every night of the week. I never get tired of it. So, that, all by itself, makes Sunday my favorite day of the week. I get to go to church twice.

This morning was a special day at church. Ed preached and I always love that. He preached a sermon that he had preached at another church a few months ago. I had a copy of that tape, so I knew what he was going to say. This time around, he said it better. I love hearing him preach. I wish you could hear him. You love words and so does he. He's a natural comedian and so are you. I think you'd enjoy hearing him.

I love the fellowship at my church. It's a small enough church that everyone knows everyone. They've become my friends. Many of them have been in my kitchen. The term "church family" means something to me.

A friend who isn't a member of my church came to the service this morning [Shirley]. She's been there several times and I'm always glad when she comes. She is searching for something better and I hope she'll find it with us.

She likes Ed and Paula, so we all went out for lunch later. I like that about Sundays, too. We usually eat together after the morning service, either just us or with other people. Sometimes I have people for lunch here at my house.

And then it's naptime. Sunday truly is a day of rest for me.

Now I'll go back to church for the evening service and it'll be different than the morning service. There aren't usually many visitors at the PM service, so it's just church family, more laid back, more "free."

Those are some of the reasons I love Sundays. It's full of my favorite things...church, church family, "real" family, friends, food, nap. But Sundays are free of some of the things that I dislike...there's no mail, the junk e-mail is less, and even the phone doesn't ring unless it's someone I love. It's free of the busyness of life during the week.

So your sweet note was perfect to receive today. I wish you could share the peace of a Sunday with me. The day relaxes me, but it also invigorates me. It gives me peace, but it gives me excitement also.

Does any of that make sense? Thank you for listening to yet another ramble. I love you, my sweet friend.

Marilyn

Paula ended her tribute with this:

Marilyn,

You were so many different things to so many different people. You were a mother, a grandmother, a sister and a friend to anyor

that needed you to fill that void in their life. You were a counselor, a babysitter, a life saver (literally) a humble servant and a strength to all who have needed you. You have given so much of yourself to all of us who knew you and needed you. There will be a huge void in so many lives. We will always miss you with all of our hearts! You were my best friend. We love you!
   Paula

Pastor Yonts preached a beautiful eulogy for the next twenty minutes. Finally, in preparing to close the service, he asked me to come and sing one final song. Of all the choruses I could have chosen, none was more appropriate than *How Great Thou Art—* Marilyn's most and least favorite song.

But this time, instead of her being distracted by the singer, I believe she was able to worship without hindrance, free of all earthly distraction, basking in the presence of Almighty God. And although still bound by worldly constraints, I was able to freely worship—my hands lifted toward heaven—in the liberty and joy of the Holy Ghost and knowledge that God had performed so many great miracles in Marilyn's life.

Then sings my soul, my Savior God to Thee. . .

It was a fitting end to her life—that God should be glorified and lifted up. When I first met Marilyn, God was unbelievable, unknowable and undesirable to her. I had watched with joy as the walls of doubt that imprisoned her were razed—slowly, but surely— and a bulwark of faith was erected in their place. She overcame the stumbling blocks that life had cast in her way. When the joy of the Lord lifted her above them, they become stepping stones.

Her God consciousness had gone from regarding Him as a dogma, creed, philosophy, religion, and ideology to intimately knowing Him and being gloriously filled with His Spirit. She had gone from loathing what Jesus Christ represents, to her soul longing after His presence.

Marilyn—once an atheist—hungered after God's holiness, and His righteousness had miraculously become the desire of her heart.

How great Thou art. . .

And how fitting was it that the very last words she uttered in this life were words of prayer to God? Very fitting, indeed.

How great Thou art.

Sunday, December 22, 2002

How strange it was to be back in the pulpit preaching on a Sunday morning and not seeing Marilyn sitting next to Paula. She'd been gone for three weeks.

I was concerned about my emotions—my first priority was to feed the people—they didn't deserve a pitiable sermon from a man in mourning. But in an unusual and unexpected way, I felt like Marilyn was there, supporting me, encouraging me. There was only one way to explain it—Shirley.

Shirley had been faithfully attending church since Marilyn died; and, as I looked out over the congregation, there she was again, sitting next to Paula. Shirley portrayed such an uncanny and striking resemblance to Marilyn that it helped me feel as though Marilyn had never left me. For weeks now I debated asking Shirley if she would allow me to take Marilyn's place in the Bible study. I kept waiting for just the right moment, but it never came. We were only just getting to know her when Marilyn died, and I wasn't sure how comfortable she would be with the idea. Yet, she was blessing me by her presence, a surrogate of sorts for the birth mother I had so recently lost.

After giving the altar call, I stepped down off the platform to go talk to her. She had that tender look in her eye, ready to hug me. As usual, I preached hard and was damp all the way through. By now I had learned, it probably wasn't going to make any difference to mention that fact. I didn't even bother to warn her. Shirley immediately reached out, embracing me in a bear hug—the kind I remembered receiving from Marilyn the first time she came to hear me preach. Her affection so moved me that it compelled me to speak my heart.

"Let me tell you something," I said, separating myself so I could look into her teary eyes. "The first time Marilyn came to hear me preach, I walked off the platform soaking wet. When I walked up to her she was ready to hug me so I backed away and said, 'Oh no, you don't want to touch me, I'm soaking wet.' But that didn't matter to her—she did it anyway. Do you realize you did the *exact* same thing just now?"

"Really?" she asked, pleasantly surprised.

"Really. And you know what else? I was a little worried about what it was going to be like preaching so soon after she died—but every time I looked out, I saw you sitting in the same spot that she used to, and you reminded me so much of her that it blessed me and strengthened me," I said, choking back tears. "Thank you *so much* for being here today and for helping me," I said softly. We held each other in another long embrace.

"Oh, and one more thing," I said. "You know how you and Marilyn were going to do that Bible study together?"

"Yes," she answered, curiously.

"Well, I feel really bad that you two were not able to do it," I said. "And I'd be honored if you'd allow me to take her place."

Shirley gave a little chuckle and smiled at me with the look of a child about to reveal a secret.

"I was hoping you would ask me that." she said, grinning.

Lord, you've opened up another window. I thought. *Perhaps the last chapter of this story has not been written after all!*

Epilogue

December 1, 2003
Appleton, Wisconsin

*M*arilyn has been gone for one year. Hard to believe, it has passed so quickly. This afternoon I went to visit her gravesite for the first time. It was a pilgrimage that was inevitable, but one I had no desire to make since the funeral. That is, until today. On the way I drove past the small duplex where she lived—and died—summoning memories that I've worked twelve months to suppress. Forcing myself to remember her death in all its surrealism served to remind me of its reality—a feeble attempt at chasing away the remnant of shock and denial that still lingers.

Marilyn's buried in a tiny Jewish cemetery in the midst of the hustle and bustle of the city. It's surrounded by old, residential homes and asphalt parking lots that hold the many vehicles of workers of the large paper mill across the street. A paved road, barely one-vehicle wide, winds through the cemetery, meandering between large, mature hardwood and cedar trees that provide a canopy of shade over the small park. Dates on some of the headstones are over 100 years old. It's a peaceful resting-place that looks like the city grew up around it.

It was a bright and sunny day. Huge trees muffled the sounds of traffic beyond the gate. A brisk wind howled through the tree tops, causing them to sway vigorously in the breeze. Large, black crows, perched in the branches above, cawed loudly, disquieting the sacredness of the moment. I stood over her grave, which is set along side Danny's, feeling an emotional numbness caused by the residue of shock at her sudden passing. Within minutes, the cold penetrated my coat, chilling me, forcing me to retreat into the warmth of my truck.

There is so much I wish I could tell her: all the people that showed up at the funeral home to pay their respects, the beauty of her memorial service, the pain that her passing has brought to all of us, and the new relationships that have resulted from it—ones she had prayed for so hard. But most of all, I wish I could share with her the result of the labor of love that she started—a victory she would be able to identify with . . .

It occurred exactly four months and one day after she died. I had started the Bible study with Shirley just after the New Year holidays were over. Without realizing it, Shirley had seated herself in the same spot at our dining room table that Marilyn had before her. Week after week, we plowed deeply through the Word of God. Again, as it always does, the Word required a response from the workman attempting to rightly divide the truth.

Tonight Shirley was being baptized in Jesus' Name for the remission of her sins—a brand new creature—a brand new start. Arriving at this night had not been easy for Shirley. She had needed to answer the same tough questions about her faith and beliefs that Marilyn did—but the reward for diligently seeking Him was about to pay off. It was the next chapter being written in a story of perpetual miracles, due in large part to our study two nights before.

I was teaching Shirley on the doctrine of baptism. She was wearing a mask of skepticism when suddenly she replied, "I'm not sure I believe this is what I'm supposed to do!"

"Why don't we take a look at all the examples in the New Testament where people are baptized and see *what* is done and *how* it's done?"

"Okay, fine," she agreed.

I began reading, just like I had with Marilyn, as well as many others before her, in the second chapter of the book of Acts, explaining each scripture, verse-by-verse. Shirley listened intensely, stone faced.

"Show me another one!" she insisted when I was done with the first example.

I turned to the next example in the eighth chapter. Shirley remained silent until I finished reading.

"Another one!"

Again, I repeated the exercise in the tenth chapter.

"Another one!"

The nineteenth chapter.

"Another one!"

Finally, after reading in the twenty-second chapter about the Apostle Paul telling of his personal conversion, I leaned back to wait for her response. Shirley was quiet. Then tears began to fall down her cheeks.

"I came here tonight prepared to quit coming to church because I knew what you were going to teach about baptism and I didn't agree with it. But I promised myself at the beginning of the year to try to do a better job of following through with things I start, so I decided to at least keep coming to the Bible study. I had no idea this was going to happen," Shirley said, starting to sob.

"I see it. I see it," she said, incredulously, "I understand now why God has been dealing with me for the past couple of years about being baptized. What should I do?"

It was one those special moments when truth triumphs, lifting the veil of confusion the devil uses to blind the eyes of human beings desperately in need of God's promises.

"That's got to be your decision," I said, "but if you know you need to be baptized, I wouldn't wait long."

Two nights later, the victory would belong to Shirley as she rose up out of the waters of baptism to walk in newness of life! Marilyn would have been overjoyed!

December 25, 2003—Christmas Day
Sturgeon Bay (Door County), Wisconsin

I didn't plan to be writing the last few paragraphs of this book in Door County. It just worked out that way. It's been a long, hard year on my family so we decided to go away for Christmas—to be together—just the four of us. When we chose to spend our vacation in this part of Wisconsin, we thought that the book would be completed. But just like everything else in this story, I'm not surprised by the irony of finishing it in the county where my birth mother grew up—a place where I have an innumerable number of relatives living and where Marilyn and my family would create some of our fondest memories.

It's one of the most beautiful places in the state—the perfect setting to reminisce. Driving through Sturgeon Bay, past *The Farm,* winding through Jacksonport, Cave Point, and Bailey's Harbor on the Lake Michigan side, making our way over to Ephraim and back down through Fish Creek and Egg Harbor on the Green Bay side, I considered all the miracles that Marilyn and my family shared in our short three years together.

One happened only recently. For the past six months, an eight inch stack of Marilyn's e-mails have been piled on my desk, used in the writing of this book. One night, for no apparent reason, I split the stack in half, like a deck of cards, and looked at the first piece of paper showing on top. It was a letter that I didn't recognize having used in the book. The letter was written by Marilyn to me, but there was a misprint—it was dated one week *after* her death.

She talked about giving me a book, as a gift, that her father owned. She fondly remembered him reading it on many occasions. The author, Zane Grey, was his favorite. Because of my love of reading, she wanted me to have it as a small token of his memory. I could not remember ever having received such a gift or seeing the book.

Paula went to the computer to research when the letter was written. The date was automatically recorded when the file was saved. It revealed she had written the letter on November 12, 2002—a little over two weeks before she died. It now made sense. The date was not a mistake. Marilyn intended to give me the book, accompanied by the letter, on the third anniversary of the night we met, when we planned to have a quiet celebration dinner. She didn't live long enough for that to happen.

I spoke with Joe and David and asked if they had seen such a book since we had cleaned out her duplex. They had not. Worse yet, so many of Marilyn's things that had been leftover, had been given away after everyone claimed the items of sentimental value. More than likely the book was sitting in the back room of a thrift shop somewhere in town. My heart sank.

A month later, just before Christmas, David called. The previous night, he could not sleep. After tossing back and forth for hours, he went downstairs to find something to read, hoping it would make him sleepy. The bookshelf was packed, especially now that he had added the many books he inherited from his mother. One, in particular, caught his attention: *Tappan's Burro*. The author was Zane Grey.

David removed the tattered, eighty-year-old, hardcover book, from the shelf. When he opened the cover, it revealed a small envelope. Turning over the envelope, it read: *Ed,* in a script that was as familiar to him as his own. Taking his liberty, he opened the envelope and removed the letter . . .

Dear Ed,

In a conversation a few days ago, someone asked, "What fun things do you remember from your childhood?" I didn't have to think for one second about my answer. I said, "It's books. Lots of books. All my spending money went to books. It's still my biggest extravagance."

I got that "reading gene" from my father. When I think of my father, I think of him sitting in his rocking chair, reading. He'd read anything. I remember him reading from the encyclopedia. He'd open it to any subject and read. But his favorite subject was history.

For many years, my Christmas, birthday and Father's Day gifts to him were books. I'd collect them all year so that I'd always have a stack of them ready to give to him on those occasions. When he died, and his belongings were split up among us, the only thing I asked for were some of the books I had given him. Those books were almost the only books I kept when I sold my house . . .

I'm giving this book to you because you inherited the "reading gene" from your grandfather, just as I did. I love that about you, Ed. It's one of the things that made you seem "familiar" to me when we met.

I'm not giving this book to you because it's great literature. I'm giving it to you because, of everything that I have of his, this is what reminds me the most of him. I'm giving it to you because I think you'll take care of it. I'm giving it to you because I see something of him in you.

I'm giving it to you because I love you.
Marilyn

Tappan's Burro now has a special place on my bookshelf: one, because it's so old and delicate, and two, because it's the last gift Marilyn ever gave me—received a year after her death. She was right—it's not great literature, but the book is priceless to me. And the way I received it?—well, another miracle, in the long line of miracles in this story.

It should have been legally impossible for me to see my adoption file twenty years ago—but I did. What were the odds of my not only growing up in the same city, but only a mile from Marilyn's house? Small, but it happened. How could Paula possibly know that the day before God prompted her to call Marilyn, that Marilyn had taken off her wedding ring for the first time, ready to begin a new life after the death of her husband? There was no way Paula could have known.

And who would have expected that the darkest event in her life would become the very thing to bring her the Light she needed most? Certainly none of us. There were miracles every step of the way.

Marilyn traded her regret for grace, her shame for forgiveness, and her guilt for mercy. The heavy burden she carried for thirty-four years was lifted by the light burden and easy yoke of Jesus Christ and was reflected in her letters . . .

Marilyn's letter to her friend, Lori—

I don't know what the next chapter of this story will be, and for right now, I'm just enjoying the present. I'm happy about so many things. I'm happy that Ed and Paula and Jordan and Jonathan are in my life. I'm happy Paula decided to make a phone call on the day she did...I'm happy Joe and David are the kind of people they are. I'm happy that everyone else in this story has embraced me and this experience we're all sharing. I'm happy that my life is the way it is today.

...if I had it in my power to change the past, to relive my life without that black part in it, and it meant giving up what I have now, I WOULDN'T change anything. The present is worth the past.

There's no doubt that the astronauts of Apollo 13 deeply regretted missing out on the rare chance to land on the moon. The incredible fear they must have felt, knowing that they had one small window of opportunity to get back to earth safely, was surely mixed with sadness because of the misfortune of their mission and bitter disappointment over what might have been. But in the end, a series of miracles gave them back their lives.

Bad things happen as we traverse this life. We plan for and expect great things to happen. We look forward to what the future holds for each one of us. We plan for success, happiness, and fulfillment. We go after it with eager anticipation. We don't plan for tragedy, but when it comes, we require a miracle. There is a scripture in the book of Romans that says, *For I reckon that the sufferings of this present time are not worthy to be compared with the glory which shall be revealed in us.*

True, Marilyn never planned on the dark event that she experienced at a young age. She never asked for it. She certainly never deserved it. But it happened. Yet, her own words testify to the fact that when a person finds Jesus Christ, they find the Healer of the brokenhearted, the Restorer of spiritually blinded eyes, and a Deliverer that sets at liberty them that are bruised by life's hardships.

In the end, no matter how bad the past, He can turn disaster into deliverance and messes into miracles. And when a person's past life is weighed in the balance with the present, they can look back and realize with confidence—in spite of what they've been through—that it's all been worth it, compared to what they have now.

Marilyn, now more than ever, I believe knows that the sufferings in this life cannot compare to the glory of the home where she now resides. She is in a place my soul longs to be. One day, by the grace of God, I will dance around the throne of glory together with her— the throne of the One that brought about all the miracles we experienced—the throne of the One that adopted us both by His Spirit.

For what is your life? It is even a vapor that appeareth for a little time, and then vanisheth away.

No, I don't feel cheated that I only had three years together with her—I feel blessed. It won't be long and soon I'll be together with Marilyn again. We may have been separated at birth, and again at death, but I can say, with the confidence of one who has seen a few miracles in my short lifetime, our next reunion will last for an eternity.

The Story of a Modern Day Miracle!

When you do what you can do, God will do what only God can do.

For information on how to order this book, you can contact Jack E. Yonts II at:

329 Lopas St.
Menasha, WI 54952

920.734.5588

jyonts2@aol.com

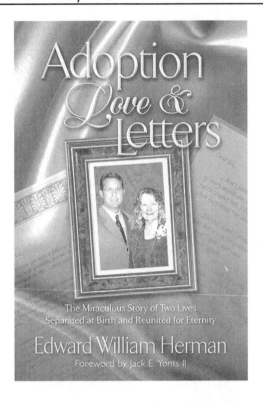

To Order *Adoption, Love & Letters* Online, Go to:

www.anointedquill.com

Contact Edward William Herman at:
Anointed Quill Publications
1767 Sandy Lane
Menasha, WI 54952
920.749.0856
or: **eherman@anointedquill.com**

There's peace + love in my ♥
& Joy + forgiveness surrounding my ♥
Soul
I know I'm forgiven, Hands open wide
And now I'm going for a
Brandnew ____